Table of Co

- I. Introduction
    1. Outcomes & Indicators 3
    2. Stories 7
    3. Songs 16
    4. Games & Activities 19
    5. Crafts 31
- II. Signs
    1. Home 50
    2. Family 68
    3. Pet 85
    4. Holiday 98
    5. Transportation 116
- III. Handouts 141
- IV. Index 157

Copyright © 2008 Time to Sign, Inc.

Family, Home, Holidays, & Transportation

Outcomes & Indicators

The Child Outcomes and indicators are depicted as follows:
Domain
    Domain Element
        Indicators

A. Language Development
A.1 Listening & Understanding
- A.1.a. Sign language naturally demonstrates increased ability to understand and participate in conversations, stories, songs, rhythms, and games
- A.1.b. Sign language assists in the understanding and following of simple and multiple-step directions
- A.1.c. Sign language greatly increases children's receptive vocabulary
- A.1.d. Sign language assists non-English-speaking children in learning to listen to and understand English as well sign language

A.2 Speaking & Communication
- A.2.a. Sign language assists in developing increasing abilities to understand and use sign language and English to communicate information, experiences, ideas, feelings, opinions, needs, and questions for other purposes
- A.2.b. Sign language instruction teaches children the use of an increasingly complex and varied signed and spoken vocabulary
- A.2.c. Sign language assists non-English speaking children in signing and speaking English

B. Literacy
B.1 Phonological Awareness
As teachers say and sign words together it serves as another way for children to understand and remember both the sign and the spoken word. When taught together sign instruction assists in providing the following benefits.
- B.1.a. Progresses in recognizing matching sounds in familiar words, songs, rhythms, games, stories, and other activities
- B.1.b. Associates sounds with written and signed words
- B.1.c. Children's use of sign language enhances language acquisition
- B.1.d. Children's learning of sign language simultaneously with words assist in like word differentiation of emergent readers

B.2 Book Knowledge & Appreciation
- B.2.a. Signing is an enjoyable activity for children that greatly enhances vocabulary, which makes learning to read easier and sometimes earlier
- B.2.b. Children who are taught sign language demonstrate progress in abilities to retell, using sign words, stories from books and personal experiences
- B.2.c. Children who are taught sign language demonstrate progress in abilities to

Copyright © 2008 Time to Sign, Inc.

act out stories in dramatic play which is a natural extension of the hand and finger movements learned in sign language

B.3 Print Awareness and Concepts
- B.3.a. Children who learn to sign develop a growing understanding of the different functions of forms of print such as signs, letters, and numbers
- B.3.b. When written words are presented with the verbal and sign introduction/instruction children better learn to recognize a word as a unit of print

B.4 Early Writing
- B.4.a. Begins to represent stories and experiences through signs, pictures, songs, games, and in play

B.5 Alphabet Knowledge
- B.5.a. Shows progress in associating the names of letters with their signs, shapes, and sounds
- B.5.b. Identifies all the letters of the alphabet, especially those in their own name
- B.5.c. Knows that the letters of the alphabet are a special category of visual graphics that can be individually signed and named

C. Mathematics

C.1 Number & Operations
- C.1.a. Children are taught the sign language counterparts to the numbers
- C.1.b. Children count numbers to assist with the retention of the number they have reached
- C.1.c. Signing assists with children's ability to count beyond the number 10
- C.1.d. Signing assists with children's learning to make use of one-to-one correspondence in counting objects and matching numbers of groups of objects

C.2 Geometry & Spatial Sense
- C.2.a. Signing assists with the recognition and ability to describe common shapes as shape signs accurately represent common shapes such as square, triangle, or circle
- C.2.b Signing assists children in developing visual and spatial awareness

D. Science

D.1 Scientific Skills & Methods
- D.1.a. Signing assists children in the understanding of scientific principles such as being able to express differences (such as big/little, open/closed, and more/less)
- D.1.b. Signing assists in increasing children's awareness
- D.1.c. Singing assists in the growing awareness of ideas and language related to time

D.2 Scientific Knowledge
- D.2.a. Signing assists in increasing awareness and beginning understanding of changes in material and cause-effect relationships
- D.2.b. Signing assists in increasing awareness of ideas and language related to time

Copyright © 2008 Time to Sign, Inc.

Family, Home, Holidays, & Transportation

and temperature
- D.2.c. Signing assists in expanding knowledge of and respect for their body and the environment
- D.2.d. Signing enhances children's abilities to observe, describe and discuss the natural world, materials, living things, and natural processes

E. Creative Arts

E.1 Music
- E.1.a. As children sign to music they develop increased interest and enjoyment in listening, singing, signing, finger plays, games, and performances

E.2 Movement
- E.2.a. Children express through sign what is felt and heard in music

E.3 Dramatic Play
- E.3.a. Children express themselves dramatically through signing

F. Social & Development

F.1 Self Concept
- F.1.a. Begins to develop and express awareness of self in terms of specific abilities, characteristics and preferences through the use of signing, for example they learn to sign their name and are given a sign name they feel reflects their personality
- F.1.b. Children's successful use of sign language enhances their confidence and self-esteem

F.2 Self Control
- F.2.a. Through the use of sign language children learn to express their feelings, emotions, needs, and opinions in everyday and in difficult situations without harming themselves, others, or property
- F.2.b. Through the use of sign language children demonstrate increased capacity to follows rules and routines, and to use materials purposefully, safely and respectfully
- F.2.c. Children's use of sign language raises communication awareness, enabling them to better tell and understand how their actions and words effect others
- F.2.d. Children's and teacher's use of sign language lowers children's noise levels in the classroom enhancing the learning atmosphere
- F.2.e. Children's use of sign language teaches them to pay better attention, they need to pay attention visually, rather than just listen
- F.2.f. Children's use of sign language increase their use of manners, which can help to eliminate potential misbehavior reactions
- F.2.g Children's use of sign language fosters an atmosphere in which children ask questions before acting, for example asking if their classmate is done with the toy before taking it and angering their classmate
- F.2.h. Classroom usage of sign language engages the teachers to be present with the child, they need to be making regular eye contact and can better see in the faces of children if anything is wrong, the child is unhappy, etc.

Copyright © 2008 Time to Sign, Inc.

F.3 Cooperation
- F.3.a. Children's use of sign language increases their abilities to sustain interactions with peers through the use of manners, enabling them to express their feelings and emotions, by helping, and by sharing
- F.3.b. Children's use of sign language increases their abilities to use compromise and discussion in playing and resolving conflicts with classmates
- F.3.c. Children's use of sign language increases their abilities to give and take in interactions; to take turns in games or using materials; and to be participatory in activities while not being overly aggressive

F.4 Social Relationships
- F.4.a. Children's use of sign language increases their signing and speaking with and accepting guidance and directions from a wide range of familiar adults
- F.4.b. Children and teacher's use of sign language in the classroom enables all in the classroom to develop friendships with peers, this is particularly true and key for any special needs members of the class.
- F.4.c. Children's use of sign language teaches them to be especially aware when classmates are in need, upset, hurt, or angry; and in expressing empathy for others

F.5 Knowledge of Families & Communities
- F.5.a. The Young Children's Signing Program incorporates family signs to assist in children's understanding of family composition
- F.5.b. The Young Children's Signing Program incorporates gender signs, boy and girl, to assist in children's understanding of genders

G. Approaches to Learning

G.1 Initiative & Curiosity
- G.1.a. Children's use of sign language increases participation in an increasing variety of tasks and activities
- G.1.b. Children's use of sign language enhances their use of imagination and inventiveness in participation in tasks and activities

G.2 Engagement & Persistence
- G.2.a Children's learning of sign language also assist them as they increase their capacity to maintain concentration over time on a task, question, or set of directions or interactions

G.3 Reasoning & Problem Solving
- G.3.a. Children's learning and use of sign language assists in the recognition and problem solving through active exploration, including trial and error, and interactions and discussions with classmates and adults

H. Physical Health & Development

H.1. Fine Motor Skills
- H.1 a. Children's learning of sign language develops hand and arm strength and dexterity needed to control such instruments as a hammer, scissors, tape, and a stapler

Family, Home, Holidays, & Transportation

- H.1.b. Children's learning of sign language develops hand-eye coordination required for use of building blocks, putting puzzles together, reproducing shapes and patterns, stringing beads, and using scissors
- H.1.c. Children's learning of sign language develops drawing and art tools such as pencils, crayons, markers, chalk, paint brushes, and computers
- H.1.d. Children's learning of sign language enables them to be able to pick up small objects

H.2 Gross Motor Skills
- H.2.a. Children's learning of sign language coordinates movements in throwing, catching, and bouncing balls

H.3 Health Status & Practices
- H.3.a. Children's learning of sign language enhances their ability to communicate health and hygiene problems to adults
- H.3.b. Children's learning of sign language enhances their knowledge of health and hygiene

Stories

Abuela by Arthur Dorros (family)
Topical signs to be learned: grandmother, bus, city, mother, Spanish, go, park, beautiful, bird, fly, where, come, look, good morning, over, sea, sailboat, banana, cousin, like, airplane, careful, uncle, aunt, more, cloud, cat, bear, chair, rest, house, father, work, hello, walk, love.
Indicators: A.1.a, A.1.b, A.1.c, A.1.d, A.2.a, A.2.b, A.2.c, B.1.a, B.1.b, B.1.c, B.1.d, B.2.a, B.2.b, B.2.c, B.3.a, B.3.b, B.4.a, C.2.b, F.1.b, F.2.d, F.2.e, F.2.h, F.5.a, G.1.a, G.1.b, G.2.a, H.1.a, H.1.b.

The Berenstain Bears We Are A Family by Stan & Jan Berenstain (family)
Topical signs to be learned: Mama, papa, sister, brother, family, daughter, son, aunt, uncle, cousin, grandfather, grandmother, love, each, other
Indicators: A.1.a, A.1.b, A.1.c, A.1.d, A.2.a, A.2.b, A.2.c, B.1.a, B.1.b, B.1.c, B.1.d, B.2.a, B.2.b, B.2.c, B.3.a, B.3.b, B.4.a, C.2.b, F.1.b, F.2.d, F.2.e, F.2.h, F.5.a, G.1.a, G.1.b, G.2.a, H.1.a, H.1.b.

A Chair for My Mother By Vera B. Williams (family (available in Spanish & Bilingual/Hmong)
Topical signs to be learned: mother, work, restaurant, school, meet, boss, clean, pay, money, fill, home, change (money), count, laugh, tired, a lot (many), little, grandma, save, buy, chair, beautiful, soft, best, fire, come, fire truck, neighbor, run, uncle, where, aunt, cat, safe, empty, move, bring, table, bed, grandpa, sister, cousin, teddy bear, thank you, hurt, heavy, bank, find, sit.
Indicators: A.1.a, A.1.b, A.1.c, A.1.d, A.2.a, A.2.b, A.2.c, B.1.a, B.1.b, B.1.c, B.1.d, B.2.a, B.2.b, B.2.c, B.3.a, B.3.b, B.4.a, C.2.b, F.1.b, F.2.d, F.2.e, F.2.f, F.2.h, F.5.a, G.1.a, G.1.b, G.2.a, H.1.a, H.1.b.

A Child's Good Night Prayer by Grace Maccarone (home, family)
Topical signs to be learned: bless, moon, stars, night, light, cars, trucks, table, bears, bunny, mouse, family, house, pillow, bed, me, toes, head, water, earth, air, children, everywhere.

Copyright © 2008 Time to Sign, Inc.

Family, Home, Holidays, & Transportation

Indicators: A.1.a, A.1.b, A.1.c, A.1.d, A.2.a, A.2.b, A.2.c, B.1.a, B.1.b, B.1.c, B.1.d, B.2.a, B.2.b, B.2.c, B.3.a, B.3.b, B.4.a, C.2.b, F.1.b, F.2.d, F.2.e, F.2.h, F.5.a, G.1.a, G.1.b, G.2.a, H.1.a, H.1.b.

Counting Kisses by Karen Katz (home, family)
Topical signs to be learned: tired, baby, kiss, numbers 1-10, little, laugh, toes, feet, knees, loud, tickle, quick/fast, nose, warm, hands, ear, gentle, eyes, last/final, head, time, bed.
Indicators: A.1.a, A.1.b, A.1.c, A.1.d, A.2.a, A.2.b, A.2.c, B.1.a, B.1.b, B.1.c, B.1.d, B.2.a, B.2.b, B.2.c, B.3.a, B.3.b, B.4.a, C.1.a, C.1.b, C.1.d, C.2.b, F.1.b, F.2.d, F.2.e, F.2.h, F.5.a, G.1.a, G.1.b, G.2.a, H.1.a, H.1.b.

December by Eve Bunting (homeless, home, family)
Topical signs to be learned: mother, live, house, made, small, Christmas, tree, spoon, star, cookie, candle, fire, coat, dad, December, sing, sleep, listen, move, tomorrow, who, hat, come, in, cold, careful, beautiful, hungry, eat, smile, share, love, merry/happy, dream, change, work.
Indicators: A.1.a, A.1.b, A.1.c, A.1.d, A.2.a, A.2.b, A.2.c, B.1.a, B.1.b, B.1.c, B.1.d, B.2.a, B.2.b, B.2.c, B.3.a, B.3.b, B.4.a, C.2.b, F.1.b, F.2.a, F.2.c, F.2.d, F.2.e, F.2.h, F.5.a, G.1.a, G.1.b, G.2.a, G.3.a, H.1.a, H.1.b.

Five Little Pumpkins (Scholastic (Halloween)
Topical signs to be learned: five, little, pumpkins, sitting, gate, first, one, said, oh my, getting, late, second, witches, in, air, third, we, don't, care, fourth, let's, run, fifth, ready, for, fun, ooh, went, wind, out, lights, rolled, out, sight.
Indicators: A.1.a, A.1.b, A.1.c, A.1.d, A.2.a, A.2.b, A.2.c, B.1.a, B.1.b, B.1.c, B.1.d, B.2.a, B.2.b, B.2.c, B.3.a, B.3.b, B.4.a, C.1.a, C.1.b, C.1.d, C.2.b, F.1.b, F.2.d, F.2.e, F.2.h, G.1.a, G.1.b, G.2.a, H.1.a, H.1.b.

Five Ugly Monsters by Tedd Arnold (Halloween)
Topical signs to be learned: Five, ugly, monsters, jump, bed, one, fell, bumped, head, doctor, telephone (call), said, no, more, three, two, I, the end.
Indicators: A.1.a, A.1.b, A.1.c, A.1.d, A.2.a, A.2.b, A.2.c, B.1.a, B.1.b, B.1.c, B.1.d, B.2.a, B.2.b, B.2.c, B.3.a, B.3.b, B.4.a, C.1.a, C.1.b, C.1.d, C.2.b, F.1.b, F.2.d, F.2.e, F.2.h, G.1.a, G.1.b, G.2.a, H.1.a, H.1.b.

Fly Away Home by Eve Bunting (homelessness, transportation)
Topical signs to be learned: dad, live, home, better, street, careful, catch, blue, pants, shirt, jacket, bag, see, sleep, sit, like, walk, pilot, move, stay, bird, stop, fly, happy, bathroom, milk, juice, bus, work, carry, hamburger, mom, save, money, safe, school, mad, special, cry, sing.
Indicators: A.1.a, A.1.b, A.1.c, A.1.d, A.2.a, A.2.b, A.2.c, B.1.a, B.1.b, B.1.c, B.1.d, B.2.a, B.2.b, B.2.c, B.3.a, B.3.b, B.4.a, C.2.b, F.1.b, F.2.a, F.2.c, F.2.d, F.2.e, F.2.h, F.5.a, G.1.a, G.1.b, G.2.a, G.3.a, H.1.a, H.1.b

Freight Train by Donald Crews (transportation (available bilingual)
Topical signs to be learned: train, track, red, orange, yellow, green, cow, blue, purple, black, move, go, through, city, dark, light, gone.
Indicators: A.1.a, A.1.b, A.1.c, A.1.d, A.2.a, A.2.b, A.2.c, B.1.a, B.1.b, B.1.c, B.1.d, B.2.a,

Family, Home, Holidays, & Transportation

B.2.b, B.2.c, B.3.a, B.3.b, B.4.a, C.2.b, F.1.b, F.2.c, F.2.d, F.2.e, F.2.h, G.1.a, G.1.b, G.2.a, H.1.a, H.1.b

<u>Good Night Moon</u> by Margaret Wise Brown (home)
Topical signs to be learned: green, room, telephone, red, balloon, picture, cow jumping, over, moon, three, little bears sit, chairs, two, kittens, mittens, toy, house, mouse, quiet, lady, goodnight, light, clock, socks, comb, brush, mush, stars, air, noise, everywhere.
Indicators: A.1.a, A.1.b, A.1.c, A.1.d, A.2.a, A.2.b, A.2.c, B.1.a, B.1.b, B.1.c, B.1.d, B.2.a, B.2.b, B.2.c, B.3.a, B.3.b, B.4.a, C.2.b, F.1.b, F.2.d, F.2.e, F.2.h, G.1.a, G.1.b, G.2.a, H.1.a, H.1.b.

<u>Guess How Much I Love You</u> by Sam McBratney (family)
Topical signs to be learned: bed, listen, guess, how much (many), love, you, high, think, toes, jump/hop, good, wish, like/same, river, across/over, far, sleepy, moon, kiss, good night.
Indicators: A.1.a, A.1.b, A.1.c, A.1.d, A.2.a, A.2.b, A.2.c, B.1.a, B.1.b, B.1.c, B.1.d, B.2.a, B.2.b, B.2.c, B.3.a, B.3.b, B.4.a, C.2.b, F.1.b, F.2.a, F.2.d, F.2.e, F.2.h, F.5.a, G.1.a, G.1.b, G.2.a, H.1.a, H.1.b.

<u>Hanukkah Lights, Hanukkah Nights</u> by Leslie Kimmelman
Topical signs to be learned: my, relatives, come, far away, help, celebrate, Hanukkah, family, lights, candle, tonight, first, night, aunt, sing, holiday, blessing, grandmother, sips, chicken, soup, second, third, nieces, spin dreidel, potato, latkes, sixth, kitten, plays, chocolate, money, seventh, cousins, eighth, shinning, happy, fourth, fifth.
Indicators: A.1.a, A.1.b, A.1.c, A.1.d, A.2.a, A.2.b, A.2.c, B.1.a, B.1.b, B.1.c, B.1.d, B.2.a, B.2.b, B.2.c, B.3.a, B.3.b, B.4.a, C.2.b, F.1.b, F.2.d, F.2.e, F.2.h, F.5.a, G.1.a, G.1.b, G.2.a, H.1.a, H.1.b.

<u>Happy Birthday, A Beginner Book of Sign</u> by Angela Bednarczyk & Janet
Topical signs to be learned: cards, balloons, clown, party hats, ice cream, cookies, gift, what is it?, cake, candles, happy, birthday
Indicators: A.1.a, A.1.b, A.1.c, A.1.d, A.2.a, A.2.b, A.2.c, B.1.a, B.1.b, B.1.c, B.1.d, B.2.a, B.2.b, B.2.c, B.3.a, B.3.b, B.4.a, C.2.b, F.1.b, F.2.d, F.2.e, F.2.h, F.5.a, G.1.a, G.1.b, G.2.a, H.1.a, H.1.b.

<u>Home for a Bunny</u> by Margaret Wise Brown (home, animals)
Topical signs to be learned: spring, frog, bird, leaves, flowers, eggs, bunny/rabbit, find, home, under, rock, ground, where, look for, your, ask, here, not, me, fall, water, come, no, can't, road/street, meet, yes.
Indicators: A.1.a, A.1.b, A.1.c, A.1.d, A.2.a, A.2.b, A.2.c, B.1.a, B.1.b, B.1.c, B.1.d, B.2.a, B.2.b, B.2.c, B.3.a, B.3.b, B.4.a, C.2.b, F.1.b, F.2.d, F.2.e, F.2.h, F.5.a, G.1.a, G.1.b, G.2.a, H.1.a, H.1.b.

<u>How Do Dinosaurs Say Good Night?</u> By Jane Yolen (home (available in Spanish)
Topical signs to be learned: how, say, good night, father, light, throw, teddy bear, shout/scream/roar, want, book, more, mother, fall, cry, no, try, kiss, quiet, hug.
Indicators: A.1.a, A.1.b, A.1.c, A.1.d, A.2.a, A.2.b, A.2.c, B.1.a, B.1.b, B.1.c, B.1.d, B.2.a, B.2.b, B.2.c, B.3.a, B.3.b, B.4.a, C.2.b, F.1.b, F.2.a, F.2.d, F.2.e, F.2.f, F.2.h, F.5.a, G.1.a, G.1.b, G.2.a, H.1.a, H.1.b.

Copyright © 2008 Time to Sign, Inc.

Family, Home, Holidays, & Transportation

I Fly by Anne Rockwell (transportation)
Topical signs to be learned: cousin, fly (airplane), captain, pilot, chair/seat, window, look at, big, airplane, flight attendant (sign: airplane + serve + agent), seat belt, light, welcome, enjoy, loud, up, wheels, sky, city, cloud, fast, drink, up, down, road, river, field, hill (mountain), house, little, stop, slow, good, love.
Indicators: A.1.a, A.1.b, A.1.c, A.1.d, A.2.a, A.2.b, A.2.c, B.1.a, B.1.b, B.1.c, B.1.d, B.2.a, B.2.b, B.2.c, B.3.a, B.3.b, B.4.a, C.2.b, F.1.b, F.2.d, F.2.e, F.2.f, F.2.h, F.5.a, G.1.a, G.1.b, G.2.a, H.1.a, H.1.b.

I Know an Old Lady Who Swallowed a Pie by Alison Jackson (Thanksgiving)
Topical signs to be learned: know, old, lady, eat, pie, dry, drank, Thanksgiving, salad, turkey, cake, bread, full.
Indicators: A.1.a, A.1.b, A.1.c, A.1.d, A.2.a, A.2.b, A.2.c, B.1.a, B.1.b, B.1.c, B.1.d, B.2.a, B.2.b, B.2.c, B.3.a, B.3.b, B.4.a, C.2.b, F.1.b, F.2.d, F.2.e, F.2.h, G.1.a, G.1.b, G.2.a, H.1.a, H.1.b.

If You Give A Mouse A Cookie by Laura Numeroff (home, pets (available in Spanish and Bilingual)
Topical signs to be learned: give, mouse, cookie, ask, glass, milk, straw, finished, napkin, mirror, mustache, hair, trim, scissors, broom, sweep, little, box, blanket, pillow, crawl, comfortable, read, story, pictures, draw, paper, crayons, sign, name, pen, hang, refrigerator, tape, remind, thirsty.
Indicators: A.1.a, A.1.b, A.1.c, A.1.d, A.2.a, A.2.b, A.2.c, B.1.a, B.1.b, B.1.c, B.1.d, B.2.a, B.2.b, B.2.c, B.3.a, B.3.b, B.4.a, C.2.b, F.1.b, F.2.d, F.2.e, F.2.f, F.2.h, G.1.a, G.1.b, G.2.a, G.3.a, H.1.a, H.1.b.

If You'll Be My Valentine by Cynthia Rylant (valentine's day)
Topical signs to be learned: you, my, valentine, kiss, two, three, walk, sing, talk, write, letter, hug, better, sit, read, book, frog, play, car, look, far, fly, sky, tea, cookies, orange, funny/silly, go, love, tree, world, happy, day.
Indicators: A.1.a, A.1.b, A.1.c, A.1.d, A.2.a, A.2.b, A.2.c, B.1.a, B.1.b, B.1.c, B.1.d, B.2.a, B.2.b, B.2.c, B.3.a, B.3.b, B.4.a, C.2.b, F.1.b, F.2.d, F.2.e, F.2.f, F.2.h, F.5.a, G.1.a, G.1.b, G.2.a, H.1.a, H.1.b.

Inside A House That Is Haunted by Alyssa Satin Capucilli (Halloween)
Topical signs to be learned: here, house, haunted, hand, knocked, door, outside, startled, spider, dropped, floor, inside, frightened, ghost, awoke, cried, BOO, surprising, cat, jumped, screeched, shook, bats, swooped, through, air, jolted, owl, called, Who's, There, spooked, mummy, ran, shriek, rattling, skeleton, moved, creak, monster, stomped, huge, feet, opened, heard, "Trick or Treat".
Indicators: A.1.a, A.1.b, A.1.c, A.1.d, A.2.a, A.2.b, A.2.c, B.1.a, B.1.b, B.1.c, B.1.d, B.2.a, B.2.b, B.2.c, B.3.a, B.3.b, B.4.a, C.2.b, F.1.b, F.2.d, F.2.e, F.2.f, F.2.h, G.1.a, G.1.b, G.2.a, H.1.a, H.1.b.

It's Mine by Gina & Mercer Mayer (manners)
Topical signs to be learned: baby, brother, sleep, my, bear, no, mine, mom, share, eat, popsicle, please, train, sister, play, reading, favorite, book, hide, book, drinking, cup, outside, sandbox, inside, blocks, dinosaur, rabbit, blow, bubbles, drop, blanket, doll, big, frog,
Indicators: A.1.a, A.1.b, A.1.c, A.1.d, A.2.a, A.2.b, A.2.c, B.1.a, B.1.b, B.1.c, B.1.d, B.2.a, B.2.b, B.2.c, B.3.a, B.3.b, B.4.a, C.2.b, F.1.b, F.2.a, F.2.d, F.2.e, F.2.f, F.2.h, F.5.a, G.1.a, G.1.b, G.2.a, H.1.a, H.1.b.

Family, Home, Holidays, & Transportation

Just Me and My Dad by Mercer Mayer (family)
Topical signs to be learned: camping, me, dad, car, little, tired, tent, fire, wood, boat, fish, picture, dinner, eggs, ghost, story, scared, hug, bed, read, all, night.
Indicators: A.1.a, A.1.b, A.1.c, A.1.d, A.2.a, A.2.b, A.2.c, B.1.a, B.1.b, B.1.c, B.1.d, B.2.a, B.2.b, B.2.c, B.3.a, B.3.b, B.4.a, C.2.b, F.1.b, F.2.a, F.2.d, F.2.e, F.2.h, F.5.a, G.1.a, G.1.b, G.2.a, H.1.a, H.1.b.

Just Me and My Mom by Mercer Mayer (family)
Topical signs to be learned: city, me, mom, money, tickets, train, steps, high, helped, busy, scared, museum, old, dinosaur, bones, little, show, hurt, costumes, guard, seals, show, art, pictures, tired, restaurant, lunch, hot dog, fun, big, store, clothes, toys, animal, time, go, taxi, fast, more, home.
Indicators: A.1.a, A.1.b, A.1.c, A.1.d, A.2.a, A.2.b, A.2.c, B.1.a, B.1.b, B.1.c, B.1.d, B.2.a, B.2.b, B.2.c, B.3.a, B.3.b, B.4.a, C.2.b, F.1.b, F.2.a, F.2.d, F.2.e, F.2.h, F.5.a, G.1.a, G.1.b, G.2.a, H.1.a, H.1.b.

Kiss Good Night by Amy Hest (home)
Topical signs to be learned: dark, stormy, night, P-L-U-M, street, little, white, house, bear, bed, ready, no, I, waiting, sit, favorite, book, words, blanket, red, outside, wind, friends, snuggle (hug), rain, roof, windows, milk, forget, kiss, good, again.
Indicators: A.1.a, A.1.b, A.1.c, A.1.d, A.2.a, A.2.b, A.2.c, B.1.a, B.1.b, B.1.c, B.1.d, B.2.a, B.2.b, B.2.c, B.3.a, B.3.b, B.4.a, C.2.b, F.1.b, F.2.a, F.2.d, F.2.e, F.2.h, G.1.a, G.1.b, G.2.a, G.3.a, H.1.a, H.1.b.

The Kissing Hand by Audrey Penn (home, family)
Topical signs to be learned: raccoon, forest, school, go, mother, home, you, play, friends, my, toys, read, books, swing, please, scared, love, new, wonderful, secret, nights, days, old, kiss, show, open, clean, food, dance.
Indicators: A.1.a, A.1.b, A.1.c, A.1.d, A.2.a, A.2.b, A.2.c, B.1.a, B.1.b, B.1.c, B.1.d, B.2.a, B.2.b, B.2.c, B.3.a, B.3.b, B.4.a, C.2.b, F.1.b, F.2.a, F.2.d, F.2.e, F.2.h, F.5.a, G.1.a, G.1.b, G.2.a, H.1.a, H.1.b.

Jingle Babies by Tom Arma (Christmas)
Topical signs to be learned: happy, snowman, round, fat, hat, busy, beautiful (pretty), angel, one, reindeer, candy cane, you, cookie, nice, sweet, little, Santa, bag, full, treats, stocking, me, you, surprises, under, tree.
Indicators: A.1.a, A.1.b, A.1.c, A.1.d, A.2.a, A.2.b, A.2.c, B.1.a, B.1.b, B.1.c, B.1.d, B.2.a, B.2.b, B.2.c, B.3.a, B.3.b, B.4.a, C.2.b, F.1.b, F.2.d, F.2.e, F.2.f, F.2.h, G.1.a, G.1.b, G.2.a, H.1.a, H.1.b.

Little Bear by Else Holmelund Minarik (family, home (available in Spanish)
Topical signs to be learned: little, bear, mother, cold, snow, wear (clothes), made, see, hat, outside, play, want, coat, pants, have; where, today, my, birthday, friends, cake, water, soup, carrot, potato, peas, tomato, hen/chicken, come, happy, thank you, smell, good, yes, duck, sit, wait, cat, cook, hot, for, big, beautiful, forget; go, moon, how, fly, can't, bird, jump, look for, sky, lunch, think, tree, look, like/same, earth, house; wish, cloud, boat, come on, red, car, fast, story, sleep, good night.
Indicators: A.1.a, A.1.b, A.1.c, A.1.d, A.2.a, A.2.b, A.2.c, B.1.a, B.1.b, B.1.c, B.1.d, B.2.a, B.2.b, B.2.c, B.3.a, B.3.b, B.4.a, C.2.b, F.1.b, F.2.a, F.2.d, F.2.e, F.2.h, F.5.a, G.1.a, G.1.b, G.2.a, G.3.a, H.1.a, H.1.b.

Copyright © 2008 Time to Sign, Inc.

Family, Home, Holidays, & Transportation

The Little Engine That Could by Watty Piper (transportation (available in Spanish)
Topical signs to be learned: little, train, happy, good, things, boys, girls, toy, animals, giraffe, bear, baby, elephant, clown, funny, blue, yellow, brown, see, cars, airplanes, books, eat, oranges, apples, red, milk, breakfast, diner, other, side, mountain, stop, shiny, new, engine, help, sad, strong, books, newspapers, world, old, tired, sleep (rest), blue, please, I, think, can, slow, started, up, faster, city.
Indicators: A.1.a, A.1.b, A.1.c, A.1.d, A.2.a, A.2.b, A.2.c, B.1.a, B.1.b, B.1.c, B.1.d, B.2.a, B.2.b, B.2.c, B.3.a, B.3.b, B.4.a, C.2.b, F.1.b, F.2.a, F.2.d, F.2.e, F.2.h, F.5.a, G.1.a, G.1.b, G.2.a, G.3.a, H.1.a, H.1.b.

Love You Forever by Sheila McGraw (Illustrator), Robert N. Munsch (family)
Topical signs to be learned: mother, baby, rock, song/sing, love, you, forever (always + still), like, always, long, live, mine (grow, two, years, old, ran, house, pulled, books, shelves, food, refrigerator, watch, toilet, kid, crazy, night, quiet, open door, crawled, across, room, looked, over, side, bed, picked up, boy, never, wanted, bath, grandma, visited, always, said, bad, words, sell, zoo, teenager, strange, friends, clothes, listened, music, man, home, house, town, car, drove) Words in parenthesis are used in the story. The first 6 words are repetitively used throughout the entire story and the song. Story song to teach children: "I'll Love you Forever, I'll Like you for Always, as long as I'm living my baby you'll be." The last part of the story changes the song from "baby you'll be" to "Mommy you'll be".
Indicators: A.1.a, A.1.b, A.1.c, A.1.d, A.2.a, A.2.b, A.2.c, B.1.a, B.1.b, B.1.c, B.1.d, B.2.a, B.2.b, B.2.c, B.3.a, B.3.b, B.4.a, C.2.b, F.1.b, F.2.a, F.2.d, F.2.e, F.2.h, F.5.a, G.1.a, G.1.b, G.2.a, H.1.a, H.1.b.

Millions of Cats by Wanda Gág (home, pets)
Topical signs to be learned: man, woman, live, house, flower, can't, happy, lonely, cat, look for, walk, here, there, hundred, thousand, million, choose, pretty, bring, home, white, black, grey, leave, brown, yellow, show, funny, thirsty, water, hungry, grass, see, ask, one, never, feed, fight, little, afraid, bath, milk.
Indicators: A.1.a, A.1.b, A.1.c, A.1.d, A.2.a, A.2.b, A.2.c, B.1.a, B.1.b, B.1.c, B.1.d, B.2.a, B.2.b, B.2.c, B.3.a, B.3.b, B.4.a, C.2.b, F.1.b, F.2.d, F.2.e, F.2.h, G.1.a, G.1.b, G.2.a, H.1.a, H.1.b.

Mommies Are For Counting Stars by Harriet Ziefert (family)
Topical signs to be learned: mommy, helps, count, stars, sit, kiss, boo-boo (hurt), make, better, practice, wait, home, bath, hair, puppet show (puppet + drama/act), watch (look at), take you there (drive), cooks, breakfast, thank you, excuse me, stop, go, rose, baby, big, sister, brother, marvelous.
Indicators: A.1.a, A.1.b, A.1.c, A.1.d, A.2.a, A.2.b, A.2.c, B.1.a, B.1.b, B.1.c, B.1.d, B.2.a, B.2.b, B.2.c, B.3.a, B.3.b, B.4.a, C.2.b, F.1.b, F.2.a, F.2.d, F.2.e, F.2.f, F.2.h, F.5.a, G.1.a, G.1.b, G.2.a, H.1.a, H.1.b.

Mr. Rabbit and the Lovely Present by Charlotte Zolotow (family, birthday) (available in Spanish)
Topical signs to be learned: rabbit, said, girl, want, help, mother, birthday, happy, give, nothing, like, good, what, red, no, bird, fire engine, apple, need, more, yellow, car, sun, butter, banana, green, peas, dinner, pear, blue, star, grapes, basket, thank you, good-bye.
Indicators: A.1.a, A.1.b, A.1.c, A.1.d, A.2.a, A.2.b, A.2.c, B.1.a, B.1.b, B.1.c, B.1.d, B.2.a, B.2.b, B.2.c, B.3.a, B.3.b, B.4.a, C.2.b, F.1.b, F.2.a, F.2.d, F.2.e, F.2.f, F.2.h, F.5.a, G.1.a, G.1.b, G.2.a, H.1.a, H.1.b.

Copyright © 2008 Time to Sign, Inc.

Family, Home, Holidays, & Transportation

<u>Nana Upstairs and Nana Downstairs</u> by Tomie De Paola (family, home)
Topical signs to be learned: boy, grandmother, great-grandmother (bounce hand forward one more time than in the sign "grandmother"), love, family, Sunday, bed, up, down, run, house, hello, candy, chair, talk, hat, red, people, see, cake, sleep, brush hair, beautiful, ice cream, grandfather, brother, father, uncle, snack, milk, cracker, mother, here, empty, cry, think, stars, kiss, both.
Indicators: A.1.a, A.1.b, A.1.c, A.1.d, A.2.a, A.2.b, A.2.c, B.1.a, B.1.e, B.2.a, B.2.b, B.2.c, B.2.c, B.3.a, B.4.a, H.1.a, and H.1.b

<u>The Napping House</u> by Audrey Wood (home)
Topical signs to be learned: house, nap/sleep, bed, on, grandma, child, dream, dog, cat, mouse, bite, scare/afraid, break, none.
Indicators: A.1.a, A.1.b, A.1.c, A.1.d, A.2.a, A.2.b, A.2.c, B.1.a, B.1.b, B.1.c, B.1.d, B.2.a, B.2.b, B.2.c, B.3.a, B.3.b, B.4.a, C.2.b, F.1.b, F.2.d, F.2.e, F.2.f, F.2.h, F.5.a, G.1.a, G.1.b, G.2.a, H.1.a, H.1.b.

<u>The Pain and the Great One</u> by Judy Blume (family)
Topical signs to be learned: brother, bed, mom, carry, get dressed, six, slow, father, help, bus, cry, mad, show, picture, dinner, eat, get, bath, face, clean, bathroom, take care, fun, begin, wait, read, remember, next, day, telephone, dance, sing, build, blocks, cat, understand, kiss, hug, love, better, great/wonderful, piano, like, aunt, baby, touch, friend, swim, afraid.
Indicators: A.1.a, A.1.b, A.1.c, A.1.d, A.2.a, A.2.b, A.2.c, B.1.a, B.1.b, B.1.c, B.1.d, B.2.a, B.2.b, B.2.c, B.3.a, B.3.b, B.4.a, C.2.b, F.1.b, F.2.a, F.2.d, F.2.e, F.2.h, F.5.a, G.1.a, G.1.b, G.2.a, H.1.a, H.1.b.

<u>A Ride on Mother's Back</u> by Emery & Durga Bernhard (family)
Topical signs to be learned: world, hold/hug, parents(mom + dad), need, hands, work, play, carry, children, ride, how, baby, back, cold, mountain, safe, warm, close, sleep, eat, kiss, good-bye, village/city, farmer, duck, rice, field, basket, fish, banana, fruit, neighbor, home, big, pig, rain, forest, grandfather, help, sister, camel, grass, move, frozen/ice, coat, snow, bowl, water, on, head, sun, rest, sing, grandmother, wind, girl, teach, story, river, make, dinner, stop, snake, spring, dance, balloon, throw, candy, hot, search, ready, thunder, hungry, sheep, brother, learn, family, all, plant, cook, night, bed, dream.
Indicators: A.1.a, A.1.b, A.1.c, A.1.d, A.2.a, A.2.b, A.2.c, B.1.a, B.1.b, B.1.c, B.1.d, B.2.a, B.2.b, B.2.c, B.3.a, B.3.b, B.4.a, C.2.b, F.1.b, F.2.d, F.2.e, F.2.h, F.5.a, G.1.a, G.1.b, G.2.a, H.1.a, H.1.b.

<u>Peter Cottontail</u> by Steve Nelson, Pamela R. Levy (Illustrator), Jack Rollins (Easter)
Topical signs to be learned: Easter, Green Valley, town, basket, bright, beautiful, color, egg, sweets, children, house, morning, bonnets, eat, wolf, no, fun, sing, dance, never, invite, me, give, hide, tree, wait, top, hill, roar, scared, drop, took (stole), forest, find, jelly bean, chocolate, rabbit, forget, see, missing, sad, spirit, fix, tell, stop, party, brave, smile, hunt, love.
Indicators: A.1.a, A.1.b, A.1.c, A.1.d, A.2.a, A.2.b, A.2.c, B.1.a, B.1.b, B.1.c, B.1.d, B.2.a, B.2.b, B.2.c, B.3.a, B.3.b, B.4.a, C.2.b, F.1.b, F.2.d, F.2.e, F.2.h, G.1.a, G.1.b, G.2.a, H.1.a, H.1.b.

<u>The Polar Express</u> by Chris Van Allsburg (Christmas, transportation)
Topical signs to be learned: Christmas, bed, listen, bells/ringing, friend, see, train, door, come, where, children, sing, eat, candy, hot, chocolate, drink, town, light, journey/travel, forest, mountain, snow, ice, big/huge, toy, made, look, sled, cheer, like, silver, smile, hug, first, shout, lost, house, sad, good-bye, merry/happy, small, box, name.

Family, Home, Holidays, & Transportation

Indicators: A.1.a, A.1.b, A.1.c, A.1.d, A.2.a, A.2.b, A.2.c, B.1.a, B.1.b, B.1.c, B.1.d, B.2.a, B.2.b, B.2.c, B.3.a, B.3.b, B.4.a, C.2.b, F.1.b, F.2.d, F.2.e, F.2.h, G.1.a, G.1.b, G.2.a, H.1.a, H.1.b.

Pumpkin Eye by Denise Fleming (Halloween)
Topical signs to be learned: yellow, moon, rising, soon, pie, eye, candle stick, burn/fire, trick, treat (candy), feet, line, street, down, hill, spirits, spill (come), purple, dragon, tails, unicorn, shadows, bats, cats, rags, hags (old lady), nails, bones, tigers, toes, heads, heart, Halloween.
Indicators: A.1.a, A.1.b, A.1.c, A.1.d, A.2.a, A.2.b, A.2.c, B.1.a, B.1.b, B.1.c, B.1.d, B.2.a, B.2.b, B.2.c, B.3.a, B.3.b, B.4.a, C.2.b, F.1.b, F.2.d, F.2.e, F.2.h, G.1.a, G.1.b, G.2.a, H.1.a, H.1.b.

Pumpkin Faces by Emma Rose (Halloween)
Topical signs to be learned: pumpkin, happy, sad, silly, mad, skinny, fat, dog, cat, nice, mean, Halloween, face.
Indicators: A.1.a, A.1.b, A.1.c, A.1.d, A.2.a, A.2.b, A.2.c, B.1.a, B.1.b, B.1.c, B.1.d, B.2.a, B.2.b, B.2.c, B.3.a, B.3.b, B.4.a, C.2.b, F.1.b, F.2.a, F.2.d, F.2.e, F.2.h, G.1.a, G.1.b, G.2.a, H.1.a, H.1.b.

Row Row Row Your Boat by Iza Trapani (transportation)
Topical signs to be learned: row, boat, down, stream, life, dream, happy, sunshine, family, oars, fly, clumsy, all your, might, water, splash, hold on, look, ahead, find, dam, wood, stop, eat, noisy, shore, rain, thunder, dry, hide, home, sky.
Indicators: A.1.a, A.1.b, A.1.c, A.1.d, A.2.a, A.2.b, A.2.c, B.1.a, B.1.b, B.1.c, B.1.d, B.2.a, B.2.b, B.2.c, B.3.a, B.3.b, B.4.a, C.2.b, F.1.b, F.2.d, F.2.e, F.2.h, G.1.a, G.1.b, G.2.a, H.1.a, H.1.b.

The Runaway Bunny by Margaret Wise Brown, Clement Hurd (pets)
Topical signs to be learned: little, bunny, run, away, mother, if, you, I after, fish, swim, fisherman, rock, mountain, high, above, climber, where, crocus, hidden, garden, gardener, find, bird, fly, tree, home, sailboat, sail, wind, blow, circus, trapeze, tightrope, walker, across, air, boy, house, mother, catch, arms, hug, stay, have, carrot
Indicators: A.1.a, A.1.b, A.1.c, A.1.d, A.2.a, A.2.b, A.2.c, B.1.a, B.1.b, B.1.c, B.1.d, B.2.a, B.2.b, B.2.c, B.3.a, B.3.b, B.4.a, C.2.b, F.1.b, F.2.d, F.2.e, F.2.h, F.5.a, G.1.a, G.1.b, G.2.a, H.1.a, H.1.b.

Say Boo
Topical signs to be learned: brothers, sisters, cave, mirror, little ghost, tonight, Halloween, scared, sad, flew, forest, practice, sat, tree, large, owl, branch, say, meadow, again, supposed, bridge, cry, brown, bat, down, night.
Indicators: A.1.a, A.1.b, A.1.c, A.1.d, A.2.a, A.2.b, A.2.c, B.1.a, B.1.b, B.1.c, B.1.d, B.2.a, B.2.b, B.2.c, B.3.a, B.3.b, B.4.a, C.2.b, F.1.b, F.2.d, F.2.e, F.2.h, G.1.a, G.1.b, G.2.a, H.1.a, H.1.b.

Stellaluna by Janell Cannon (family, animals) (available in Spanish)
Topical signs to be learned: forest, far, mother, fruit, bat, baby, love, name, night, fly, look for, food, owl, down, cold, afraid, where, bird, what, grasshopper, like/same, away, all, day, night, bug, taste, awful, fall, teach, bad, learn, embarrass, lost, dark, find, delicious, can't, see, safe, different, friend.
Indicators: A.1.a, A.1.b, A.1.c, A.1.d, A.2.a, A.2.b, A.2.c, B.1.a, B.1.b, B.1.c, B.1.d, B.2.a, B.2.b, B.2.c, B.3.a, B.3.b, B.4.a, C.2.b, F.1.b, F.2.d, F.2.e, F.2.h, F.5.a, G.1.a, G.1.b, G.2.a, H.1.a, H.1.b.

Copyright © 2008 Time to Sign, Inc.

Family, Home, Holidays, & Transportation

St. Patrick's Day by Gail Gibbons (St. Patrick's Day)
Topical signs to be learned: St. Patrick's Day, March, 17, holiday, world, live, year, hundred, family, name, boy, take, sheep, help, want, do, dream, teach, build, church, school, care, love, wear, green, decorate, door, window, three, leaf, magic, catch, gold, friend, make, cake, cookie, sweet, share, give, flower, act, party, fun, sing, dance, play, game, flag, hat, snake, drum, fish, sun.
Indicators: A.1.a, A.1.b, A.1.c, A.1.d, A.2.a, A.2.b, A.2.c, B.1.a, B.1.b, B.1.c, B.1.d, B.2.a, B.2.b, B.2.c, B.3.a, B.3.b, B.4.a, C.2.b, F.1.b, F.2.d, F.2.e, F.2.h, G.1.a, G.1.b, G.2.a, H.1.a, H.1.b.

Ten Days of Christmas (Wee Sign Board Book) by Pamela Conn (Christmas)
Topical signs to be learned: Holiday signs
Indicators: A.1.a, A.1.b, A.1.c, A.1.d, A.2.a, A.2.b, A.2.c, B.1.a, B.1.b, B.1.c, B.1.d, B.2.a, B.2.b, B.2.c, B.3.a, B.3.b, B.4.a, C.1.a, C.1.b, C.1.d, C.2.b, F.1.b, F.2.d, F.2.e, F.2.h, G.1.a, G.1.b, G.2.a, H.1.a, H.1.b.

Thanksgiving Story (flannel board story)
Thanksgiving Flannel Board Story –
    Our story happened long ago, before T.V. and radio.
    The pilgrims sailed the ocean gray,
    to find a brand new place to stay.
    The Indians were already here,
    planting corn and hunting deer.
    The pilgrims looked, the Indians looked,
    And they were both afraid.
    Would they fight and hurt each other?
    "No", said the Indian,
    "I will be your brother."
    So, they both planned a party gay.
    Do you know what they called it?

THANKSGIVING DAY!

Topical signs to be learned: story, past, before, T.V., radio, pilgrims, sailed, ocean, gray, find, place, stay, Indians, here, plant, corn, hunt, deer, looked, afraid, fight, hurt, each, other, No, I, brother, planned, party, you, know, what, name, Thanksgiving, Day.
Indicators: A.1.a, A.1.b, A.1.c, A.1.d, A.2.a, A.2.b, A.2.c, B.1.a, B.1.b, B.1.c, B.1.d, B.2.a, B.2.b, B.2.c, B.3.a, B.3.b, B.4.a, C.2.b, F.1.b, F.2.d, F.2.e, F.2.h, G.1.a, G.1.b, G.2.a, H.1.a, H.1.b

That's Not Fair by Gina & Mercer Mayer (home, family)
Topical signs to be learned: fair, bed, make, mom, sister, watermelon, living room, kitchen, new, clothes, toy, store, ice cream, candy, home, tent, outside, skunk, bike, ride, dog, bath, dirty, dinner, eat, carrots, dad, sorry, TV, every, night.
Indicators: A.1.a, A.1.b, A.1.c, A.1.d, A.2.a, A.2.b, A.2.c, B.1.a, B.1.b, B.1.c, B.1.d, B.2.a, B.2.b, B.2.c, B.3.a, B.3.b, B.4.a, C.2.b, F.1.b, F.2.a, F.2.d, F.2.e, F.2.f, F.2.h, G.1.a, G.1.b, G.2.a, H.1.a, H.1.b

A Turkey For Thanksgiving by Eve Bunting (Thanksgiving)
Topical signs to be learned: Thanksgiving, help, sheep, rabbit, goat, nice, friend, share,

Family, Home, Holidays, & Transportation

have, turkey, find, cold, dinner, time, come, see, river, fat, show, wait, slow, ran, try, fly, fall, happy, sit, like, how, taste, nice, on.
Indicators: A.1.a, A.1.b, A.1.c, A.1.d, A.2.a, A.2.b, A.2.c, B.1.a, B.1.b, B.1.c, B.1.d, B.2.a, B.2.b, B.2.c, B.3.a, B.3.b, B.4.a, C.2.b, F.1.b, F.2.d, F.2.e, F.2.h, G.1.a, G.1.b, G.2.a, H.1.a, H.1.b.

<u>The Very First Thanksgiving Day</u> by Rhonda Gowler Greene (Thanksgiving)
Topical signs to be learned: first, Thanksgiving, day, food, corn, berry, turkey, share, Indian, know, live, winter, eat, farm, work, learn, house, build, sun, snow, stone, boat, sea, wind, land, begin/start, travel.
Indicators: A.1.a, A.1.b, A.1.c, A.1.d, A.2.a, A.2.b, A.2.c, B.1.a, B.1.b, B.1.c, B.1.d, B.2.a, B.2.b, B.2.c, B.3.a, B.3.b, B.4.a, C.2.b, F.1.b, F.2.a, F.2.d, F.2.e, F.2.h, G.1.a, G.1.b, G.2.a, H.1.a, H.1.b.

<u>The Wheels on the Bus and Other Transportation Songs</u> (Scholastic) illustrated by Dick Witt (transportation)
Topical signs to be learned: this is a song book of various transportation songs. The songs are Daisy, Daisy; Down by the Station; I've Been Working on the Railroad; Sally Go Around the Sun; She'll be Coming Around the Mountain; Yankee Doodle; Ride a Cockhorse; Row, Row, Row, Your Boat; Wheels on the Bus
Indicators: A.1.a, A.1.b, A.1.c, A.1.d, A.2.a, A.2.b, A.2.c, B.1.a, B.1.b, B.1.c, B.1.d, B.2.a, B.2.b, B.2.c, B.3.a, B.3.b, B.4.a, C.2.b, F.1.b, F.2.d, F.2.e, F.2.h, G.1.a, G.1.b, G.2.a, H.1.a, H.1.b.

<u>Where is Alice's Bear?</u> by Fiona Pragoff (home)
Topical signs to be learned: bear, house, crib, baby carriage, car, toy, chest.
Indicators: A.1.a, A.1.b, A.1.c, A.1.d, A.2.a, A.2.b, A.2.c, B.1.a, B.1.b, B.1.c, B.1.d, B.2.a, B.2.b, B.2.c, B.3.a, B.3.b, B.4.a, C.2.b, F.1.b, F.2.d, F.2.e, F.2.h, G.1.a, G.1.b, G.2.a, H.1.a, H.1.b.

Songs

Buckle Bear Song (trans.)
Indicators: A.1.a, A.1.b, A.1.c, A.1.d, A.2.a, A.2.b, A.2.c, B.1.a, B.1.c, B.1.d, B.2.a, B.2.b, B.3.a, B.4.a, C.2.b, E.1.a, E.2.a, F.1.b, F.2.b, F.2.e, F.2.h, F.3.c, G.1.a, G.1.b, H.1.a, H.1.b, H.1.d

Camping Song (trans.)
Indicators: A.1.a, A.1.b, A.1.c, A.1.d, A.2.a, A.2.b, A.2.c, B.1.a, B.1.c, B.1.d, B.2.a, B.2.b, B.3.a, B.4.a, C.2.b, E.1.a, E.2.a, F.1.b, F.2.e, F.2.h, F.3.c, G.1.a, G.1.b, H.1.a, H.1.b, H.1.d

Car Song - (trans.)
Indicators: A.1.a, A.1.b, A.1.c, A.1.d, A.2.a, A.2.b, A.2.c, B.1.a, B.1.c, B.1.d, B.2.a, B.2.b, B.3.a, B.4.a, C.2.b, E.1.a, E.2.a, F.1.b, F.2.b, F.2.e, F.2.h, F.3.c, G.1.a, G.1.b, H.1.a, H.1.b, H.1.d

Did You Ever Go A Camping (trans.)
Indicators: A.1.a, A.1.b, A.1.c, A.1.d, A.2.a, A.2.b, A.2.c, B.1.a, B.1.c, B.1.d, B.2.a, B.2.b, B.3.a, B.4.a, C.2.b, E.1.a, E.2.a, F.1.b, F.2.e, F.2.h, F.3.c, G.1.a, G.1.b, H.1.a, H.1.b, H.1.d

Down by the Station (trans.)
Indicators: A.1.a, A.1.b, A.1.c, A.1.d, A.2.a, A.2.b, A.2.c, B.1.a, B.1.c, B.1.d, B.2.a, B.2.b, B.3.a, B.4.a, C.2.b, E.1.a, E.2.a, F.1.b, F.2.e, F.2.h, F.3.c, G.1.a, G.1.b, H.1.a, H.1.b, H.1.d

Family, Home, Holidays, & Transportation

Eight Little Candles (holidays)
Indicators: A.1.a, A.1.b, A.1.c, A.1.d, A.2.a, A.2.b, A.2.c, B.1.a, B.1.c, B.1.d, B.2.a, B.2.b, B.3.a, B.4.a, C.1.a, C.1.b, C.1.d, C.2.b, E.1.a, E.2.a, F.1.b, F.2.e, F.2.h, F.3.c, G.1.a, G.1.b, H.1.a, H.1.b, H.1.d

Five Little Pumpkins (holidays)
Indicators: A.1.a, A.1.b, A.1.c, A.1.d, A.2.a, A.2.b, A.2.c, B.1.a, B.1.c, B.1.d, B.2.a, B.2.b, B.3.a, B.4.a, C.1.a, C.1.b, C.1.d, C.2.b, E.1.a, E.2.a, F.1.b, F.2.e, F.2.h, F.3.c, G.1.a, G.1.b, H.1.a, H.1.b, H.1.d

Happy Little Child (family)
Indicators: A.1.a, A.1.b, A.1.c, A.1.d, A.2.a, A.2.b, A.2.c, B.1.a, B.1.c, B.1.d, B.2.a, B.2.b, B.3.a, B.4.a, C.2.b, E.1.a, E.2.a, F.1.b, F.2.a, F.2.e, F.2.h, F.3.c, F.5.a, G.1.a, G.1.b, H.1.a, H.1.b, H.1.d

Happy Mother's Day (family)
Indicators: A.1.a, A.1.b, A.1.c, A.1.d, A.2.a, A.2.b, A.2.c, B.1.a, B.1.c, B.1.d, B.2.a, B.2.b, B.3.a, B.4.a, C.2.b, E.1.a, E.2.a, F.1.b, F.2.e, F.2.h, F.3.c, F.5.a, G.1.a, G.1.b, H.1.a, H.1.b, H.1.d

Happy Father's Day (family)
Indicators: A.1.a, A.1.b, A.1.c, A.1.d, A.2.a, A.2.b, A.2.c, B.1.a, B.1.c, B.1.d, B.2.a, B.2.b, B.3.a, B.4.a, C.2.b, E.1.a, E.2.a, F.1.b, F.2.e, F.2.h, F.3.c, F.5.a, G.1.a, G.1.b, H.1.a, H.1.b, H.1.d

I'm a Fish (animals, pets)
Indicators: A.1.a, A.1.b, A.1.c, A.1.d, A.2.a, A.2.b, A.2.c, B.1.a, B.1.c, B.1.d, B.2.a, B.2.b, B.3.a, B.4.a, C.2.b, E.1.a, E.2.a, F.1.b, F.2.e, F.2.h, F.3.c, G.1.a, G.1.b, H.1.a, H.1.b, H.1.d

I'm a Little Dreidel (holidays)
Indicators: A.1.a, A.1.b, A.1.c, A.1.d, A.2.a, A.2.b, A.2.c, B.1.a, B.1.c, B.1.d, B.2.a, B.2.b, B.3.a, B.4.a, C.2.b, E.1.a, E.2.a, F.1.b, F.2.e, F.2.h, F.3.c, G.1.a, G.1.b, H.1.a, H.1.b, H.1.d

I'm a Little Valentine (holidays)
Indicators: A.1.a, A.1.b, A.1.c, A.1.d, A.2.a, A.2.b, A.2.c, B.1.a, B.1.c, B.1.d, B.2.a, B.2.b, B.3.a, B.4.a, C.2.b, E.1.a, E.2.a, F.1.b, F.2.e, F.2.h, F.3.c, G.1.a, G.1.b, H.1.a, H.1.b, H.1.d

I've Been Working on the Railroad (trans.)
Indicators: A.1.a, A.1.b, A.1.c, A.1.d, A.2.a, A.2.b, A.2.c, B.1.a, B.1.c, B.1.d, B.2.a, B.2.b, B.3.a, B.4.a, C.2.b, E.1.a, E.2.a, F.1.b, F.2.e, F.2.h, F.3.c, G.1.a, G.1.b, H.1.a, H.1.b, H.1.d

Jack-O-Lantern (holidays)
Indicators: A.1.a, A.1.b, A.1.c, A.1.d, A.2.a, A.2.b, A.2.c, B.1.a, B.1.c, B.1.d, B.2.a, B.2.b, B.3.a, B.4.a, C.2.b, E.1.a, E.2.a, F.1.b, F.2.e, F.2.h, F.3.c, G.1.a, G.1.b, H.1.a, H.1.b, H.1.d

Jingle Bells (holidays)
Indicators: A.1.a, A.1.b, A.1.c, A.1.d, A.2.a, A.2.b, A.2.c, B.1.a, B.1.c, B.1.d, B.2.a, B.2.b, B.3.a, B.4.a, C.2.b, E.1.a, E.2.a, F.1.b, F.2.e, F.2.h, F.3.c, G.1.a, G.1.b, H.1.a, H.1.b, H.1.d

Kwanzaa's Here (holidays)
Indicators: A.1.a, A.1.b, A.1.c, A.1.d, A.2.a, A.2.b, A.2.c, B.1.a, B.1.c, B.1.d, B.2.a, B.2.b, B.3.a, B.4.a, C.2.b, E.1.a, E.2.a, F.1.b, F.2.e, F.2.h, F.3.c, G.1.a, G.1.b, H.1.a, H.1.b, H.1.d

Copyright © 2008 Time to Sign, Inc.

Family, Home, Holidays, & Transportation

Little Red Caboose (trans.)
Indicators: A.1.a, A.1.b, A.1.c, A.1.d, A.2.a, A.2.b, A.2.c, B.1.a, B.1.c, B.1.d, B.2.a, B.2.b, B.3.a, B.4.a, C.2.b, E.1.a, E.2.a, F.1.b, F.2.e, F.2.h, F.3.c, G.1.a, G.1.b, H.1.a, H.1.b, H.1.d

Over the River and Through the Woods (family)
Indicators: A.1.a, A.1.b, A.1.c, A.1.d, A.2.a, A.2.b, A.2.c, B.1.a, B.1.c, B.1.d, B.2.a, B.2.b, B.3.a, B.4.a, C.2.b, E.1.a, E.2.a, F.1.b, F.2.e, F.2.h, F.3.c, G.1.a, G.1.b, H.1.a, H.1.b, H.1.d

Pumpkin, Pumpkin (holidays)
Indicators: A.1.a, A.1.b, A.1.c, A.1.d, A.2.a, A.2.b, A.2.c, B.1.a, B.1.c, B.1.d, B.2.a, B.2.b, B.3.a, B.4.a, C.2.b, E.1.a, E.2.a, F.1.b, F.2.e, F.2.h, F.3.c, G.1.a, G.1.b, H.1.a, H.1.b, H.1.d

Row, Row, Row Your Boat (trans.)
Indicators: A.1.a, A.1.b, A.1.c, A.1.d, A.2.a, A.2.b, A.2.c, B.1.a, B.1.c, B.1.d, B.2.a, B.2.b, B.3.a, B.4.a, C.2.b, E.1.a, E.2.a, F.1.b, F.2.e, F.2.h, F.3.c, G.1.a, G.1.b, H.1.a, H.1.b, H.1.d

Safety Belts (trans.)
Indicators: A.1.a, A.1.b, A.1.c, A.1.d, A.2.a, A.2.b, A.2.c, B.1.a, B.1.c, B.1.d, B.2.a, B.2.b, B.3.a, B.4.a, C.2.b, E.1.a, E.2.a, F.1.b, F.2.b, F.2.e, F.2.h, F.3.c, G.1.a, G.1.b, H.1.a, H.1.b, H.1.d

Stars and Stripes (holidays)
Indicators: A.1.a, A.1.b, A.1.c, A.1.d, A.2.a, A.2.b, A.2.c, B.1.a, B.1.c, B.1.d, B.2.a, B.2.b, B.3.a, B.4.a, C.2.b, E.1.a, E.2.a, F.1.b, F.2.e, F.2.h, F.3.c, G.1.a, G.1.b, H.1.a, H.1.b, H.1.d

Traffic Light (trans.)
Indicators: A.1.a, A.1.b, A.1.c, A.1.d, A.2.a, A.2.b, A.2.c, B.1.a, B.1.c, B.1.d, B.2.a, B.2.b, B.3.a, B.4.a, C.2.b, E.1.a, E.2.a, F.1.b, F.2.e, F.2.h, F.3.c, G.1.a, G.1.b, H.1.a, H.1.b, H.1.d

Transportation Song (trans.)
Indicators: A.1.a, A.1.b, A.1.c, A.1.d, A.2.a, A.2.b, A.2.c, B.1.a, B.1.c, B.1.d, B.2.a, B.2.b, B.3.a, B.4.a, C.2.b, E.1.a, E.2.a, F.1.b, F.2.e, F.2.h, F.3.c, G.1.a, G.1.b, H.1.a, H.1.b, H.1.d

We Wish You a Merry Christmas (holidays)
Indicators: A.1.a, A.1.b, A.1.c, A.1.d, A.2.a, A.2.b, A.2.c, B.1.a, B.1.c, B.1.d, B.2.a, B.2.b, B.3.a, B.4.a, C.2.b, E.1.a, E.2.a, F.1.b, F.2.e, F.2.h, F.3.c, G.1.a, G.1.b, H.1.a, H.1.b, H.1.d

Wheels on the Bus (trans.)
Indicators: A.1.a, A.1.b, A.1.c, A.1.d, A.2.a, A.2.b, A.2.c, B.1.a, B.1.c, B.1.d, B.2.a, B.2.b, B.3.a, B.4.a, C.2.b, E.1.a, E.2.a, F.1.b, F.2.e, F.2.h, F.3.c, G.1.a, G.1.b, H.1.a, H.1.b, H.1.d

Where are My Pets (family, pets)
Indicators: A.1.a, A.1.b, A.1.c, A.1.d, A.2.a, A.2.b, A.2.c, B.1.a, B.1.c, B.1.d, B.2.a, B.2.b, B.3.a, B.4.a, C.2.b, E.1.a, E.2.a, F.1.b, F.2.e, F.2.h, F.3.c, G.1.a, G.1.b, H.1.a, H.1.b, H.1.d

Windshield Wiper (trans.)
Indicators: A.1.a, A.1.b, A.1.c, A.1.d, A.2.a, A.2.b, A.2.c, B.1.a, B.1.c, B.1.d, B.2.a, B.2.b, B.3.a, B.4.a, C.2.b, E.1.a, E.2.a, F.1.b, F.2.e, F.2.h, F.3.c, G.1.a, G.1.b, H.1.a, H.1.b, H.1.d

Copyright © 2008 Time to Sign, Inc.

Family, Home, Holidays, & Transportation

Games & Activities

Boat Floats (transportation)
Materials: large shallow pan of water, sponges, scissors, one large block, 2" twigs, dish, heavy rock (optional).

Fill the pan half full of water. Cut the sponges in half. Explain that the water is ocean in water in a place called a harbor, which is a special place for boats. Let each child choose a sponge as their boat and place it in the harbor. Place the wooden block in the pan for a dock, talk about what a dock is for. Place twigs on the rug and allow each child to choose one, these are their twig people. Have them walk them along the dock and place them in their boat. Talk about places the boats and twig people might go and what they might do out in their boats on the ocean. Remove a boat and place it on a dish. Ask the children if the boat is moving and what it needs to move. Now place the boat back on the water. Boats need water. They are built to float. They provide transportation on water. Send a sponge and a twig person home with each child so they can float their boats at home and find harbors for them.

To demonstrate how boats can sink, place a sponge in a pan of water. Explain that the boat is pushing down on the water. Place on hand in the air, palm down. Move the hand towards the rug. Move the other hand, palm up, to meet the hand moving down. When the hands meet, stop. The bottom hand is the water pushing up on the boat, keeping the boat from sinking. Now place a heavy rock on the sponge. The boat is pushing down on the water with greater force and the water cannot hold it up. Place your palms together and push your top palm down to make the bottom hand sink to the floor. Take turns placing the rock on the boat and sinking it.

Topical signs to be learned: boat, water, ocean, people, move, heavy,
Indicators: A.1.a, A.1.b, A.1.c, A.1.d, A.2.a, A.2.b, A.2.c, B.1.c, B.2.a, B.2.b, B.2.c, C.2.b, F.1.b, F.2.b, F.2.c, F.2.d, F.2.e, F.2.h, F.3.a, F.3.c, F.4.a, G.1.a, G.1.b, G.2.a, G.3.a, H.1.a, H.1.d, H.2.a.

The Caboose is on the Loose (transportation)
This game can have 10-50+ players (At least three "trains" and one "caboose" needed.) Have the participants get into groups of three. If there are a few left over, they will become loose cabooses. If everyone is in a group of three, ask one group to become the loose cabooses. Make sure there is a caboose for every two or three trains. Each group of three will form a train, with on person behind another. The person behind puts his hands on the waist of the person in front. On the command "start," the trains chug around the area and the cabooses quickly seek a train to join. This means that they attach to the last person in the train by taking hold of the person's waist. When they do so, they yell "Go!" This is the signal for the engine, or the first person in the train to disconnect, thereby becoming a loose caboose. The trains move to keep this from happening, trying to dodge the cabooses. This, of course, should be done in a defined area, or you may find trains head for destinations unknown. The game goes on until players start to tire, about a few minutes.

Topical signs to be learned: group, train, caboose, 3, behind, start, join, go, first, person.
Indicators: A.1.a, A.1.b, A.1.c, A.1.d, A.2.a, A.2.b, A.2.c, B.1.c, B.2.a, B.2.b, B.2.c, C.2.b, F.1.b, F.2.b, F.2.c, F.2.e, F.2.h, F.3.a, F.3.c, F.4.a, G.1.a, G.1.b, G.2.a, H.1.d, H.2.a.

Copyright © 2008 Time to Sign, Inc.

Family, Home, Holidays, & Transportation

Car Car (transportation)
Players pair up by height (is someone is left over, there can be a group of three). Partners stand with an arm's length facing the same direction, one in front of the other. The one in the back is the driver. The car must put their arms up in from of themselves in a relaxed manner, creating bumpers. The car closes its eyes and the driver puts his hands on their shoulders and begins to guide the car carefully, avoiding crashing into other cars. After a few minutes, everyone stops and switches: car becomes driver, driver becomes car. So if you are the driver first, you had better treat your car right if you expect similar treatment. If the game gets too rough you can have "police" car introduced to stop people and give them tickets, or you could have a tow truck to tow crashed cars to the garage where they must stay for at least a minute for repairs.

Topical signs to be learned: car, other, drive, stop, people, give, police, truck, fix.
Indicators: A.1.a, A.1.b, A.1.c, A.1.d, A.2.a, A.2.b, A.2.c, B.1.c, B.2.a, B.2.b, B.2.c, C.2.b, F.1.b, F.2.b, F.2.c, F.2.e, F.2.h, F.3.a, F.3.c, F.4.a, G.1.a, G.1.b, G.2.a, H.1.d, H.2.a.

Car Wash (transportation)
Game can have 5-35 players, although for 25 or more players make more car washes as needed.

The players form two parallel lines facing each other, about 3 feet apart. They can kneel, crouch, or stand, depending on the softness of the surface and the inclination of the participants. Ask the players to practice motions a carwash makes, such as spraying, brushing, and towel drying. Then tell them that they are going to be the car wash (and the cars, for that matter). Each car/player gets an opportunity to say what kind of car he is and the kind of cleaning he needs—vigorous or gentle, depending on the condition he is in. For instance, an old Chevy that has been driving through mud will need a lot of cleaning, but a new Bentley right off the showroom floor will need only a light dusting. Just for fun, you can have a fantasy wash where players can be anything they want: a frog, a double-decker bus, even a cat on a hot tin roof. Whatever.

Topical signs to be learned: car, wash, line, stand, practice, motions (move), make, say, what, kind, clean, need, gentle, old, new.
Indicators: A.1.a, A.1.b, A.1.c, A.1.d, A.2.a, A.2.b, A.2.c, B.1.c, B.2.a, B.2.b, B.2.c, C.2.b, F.1.b, F.2.b, F.2.c, F.2.e, F.2.h, F.3.a, F.3.c, F.4.a, G.1.a, G.1.b, G.2.a, H.1.d, H.2.a.

Cardboard Carton Play (home, family, community)
Materials: large cardboard box (such as from appliances or office furniture), knife to cut cardboard (adult use only), markers, paint and brushes (optional)duct tape (optional).

Place the box on the ground. Decide what kind of structure you want such as a cave, igloo, castle, fort, house, store, etc. Draw lines for windows, doors, chimney, or other features. Cut the cardboard with a sharp knife (adult only). Push the windows and doors so they will open and close easily. Use duct tape tabs for handles or openers on doors and windows. Add signs or additional features with the marker or paint as needed. Other items can be used in the play such as books, flashlight, paper and crayons, pillows, sleeping bag, toys of all kinds.

Indicators: A.1.a, A.1.b, A.1.c, A.1.d, A.2.a, A.2.b, A.2.c, B.1.c, B.2.a, B.2.b, B.2.c, C.2.b, F.1.b, F.2.a, F.2.b, F.2.c, F.2.d, F.2.e, F.2.f, F.2.g, F.3.a, F.3.b, F.3.c, F.4.b, F.4.c, G.1.a, G.1.b, G.2.a, G.3.a, H.1.a, H.1.b, H.1.d, H.2.a.

Family, Home, Holidays, & Transportation

Choo Choo (transportation)

Trains are not only a good from of transportation, they are also good places to meet people. And on this train, you can meet a lot of people who will cheer your name.

The game starts in a circle. The leader, after explaining that it is a name game that is easier to do than to explain, starts chugging along moving and sounding like a steam engine. He stops in front of a person, asks her name, and then gives her a little cheer using her name, such as "Edna, Edna, Edna, Edna, Edna!" At the same time, he also makes body movements, which may vary with each added person. Or you can use the person's name sign in the cheer. The leader then invites the person to join the train by turning his back to her and putting her hands on this waist (or shoulders). Once a person joins the train, she can make train sounds and motions, too. When they come to the next person, they ask his name and when they hear it, they both give a cheer. That person is then asked to join and the game continues. After the train has about seven people, split the train in two. For a large group, repeat splitting as many times as necessary until everyone is given a cheer within a few minutes.

Topical signs to be learned: train, meet, circle, game, leader, ask, name, cheer, body, movement (move), join, continue (go on), next, person.
Indicators: A.1.a, A.1.b, A.1.c, A.1.d, A.2.a, A.2.b, A.2.c, B.1.c, B.2.a, B.2.b, B.2.c, C.2.b, F.1.b, F.2.b, F.2.c, F.2.e, F.2.h, F.3.a, F.3.c, F.4.a, G.1.a, G.1.b, G.2.a, H.1.d, H.2.a.

Cockpit (transportation)

Materials: box (the size of a two-drawer file cabinet), two 3-foot dowels, butcher paper, yarn, tempera paint, shallow tins for painting, paintbrushes, scissors, masking tape, glue, colored markers, pencils and crayons, sharp instrument for cutting (for adult use only).

Place the box on its side. Completely remove the bottom of the box (save this piece of cardboard for the steering yoke.) Tape the two ends of the box closed. Cut a windshield in one side of the box. Cut two holes in the front top corners of the box. Draw two airplane steering yokes on the extra cardboard and cut out. Punch holes in the center of each steering yoke, and punch four holes beneath the windshield. Align the holes on each steering yoke with the holes beneath the windshield. Tie the yokes to the box with yearn. Paint the cockpit instrument panel. Cut a long strip of butcher paper the width of the windshield. Mark lines to make sections on the butcher paper that are the same length as the windshield. Draw pictures of destinations on the sections of the butcher paper. Tape the ends of the butcher paper to the dowels, leaving space at the top of the dowel to insert into the holes in the top of the box. Insert the dowels in the holes in the top of the box and scroll. Now have fun flying your airplane!

Topical signs to be learned: airplane, box, paint, scissors, glue, pencil, crayon, draw, picture.
Indicators: A.1.a, A.1.b, A.1.c, A.1.d, A.2.a, A.2.b, A.2.c, B.1.c, B.2.a, B.2.b, B.2.c, C.2.b, E.3.a, F.1.b, F.2.a, F.2.b, F.2.c, F.2.d, F.2.e, F.2.f, F.2.g, F.3.a, F.3.b, F.3.c, F.4.b, F.4.c, G.1.a, G.1.b, G.2.a, G.3.a, H.1.a, H.1.b, H.1.d, H.2.a.

Cutting Roads (transportation)

Materials: white paper, black marker, scissors, plastic bags.

Draw lines spaced 1" apart down a sheet of white paper with a black marker. These are roads. Make at least one sheet per child. Or have older children make their own roads.

Copyright © 2008 Time to Sign, Inc.

Family, Home, Holidays, & Transportation

Give each child a sheet of roads, scissors, and a plastic bag. Trace the roads with your finger, count the roads, then have the children cut out the roads on their papers. Mark each road with the child's name or have them write their name on their roads. Have children place all the roads end to end. Make patterns with the roads, count the roads, etc. Place the roads in the plastic bag so the children can bring them home to build roads at home. You can also tape a large piece of butcher paper onto a wall and tape pieces of road onto the paper as well as pictures of cards from magazines or that children draw.

Topical signs to be learned: road/street, car, scissors, count, number signs, write, name, bring, home.
Indicators: A.1.b, A.1.c, A.1.d, A.2.a, A.2.b, A.2.c, B.1.c, C.1.a, C.1.b, C.1.d, C.2.b, F.1.b, F.2.b, F.2.c, F.2.d, F.2.e, F.2.h, F.3.c, G.1.a, G.1.b, G.2.a, G.3.a, H.1.a, H.1.b, H.1.c, H.1.d.

Dramatic Play: Baby Nursery (family)

Materials: baby dolls, baby bottles, baby blankets, doll clothes, small tub and water (optional), baby shampoo (optional), pictures of babies; doll crib or cradle toy, or make one from boxes; baby books, baby wipes, bibs, car seats, diapers (and extra tape), empty baby food jars, pacifier for dolls, real rocking chair, songs to sing, spoons and dishes; empty lotion, powder, and baby wash bottles; rattles, toy key ring, and other baby toys.

Set up a corner as a baby nursery, for newborns only, or for babies of all ages and needs. (Make cradles from cardboard boxes lined with blankets for sleepy babies.) Some of the baby activities possible might include burping, changing diapers, feeding with bottles, feeding with spoons from dishes that are filled from empty baby food jars; playing patty-cake, so-big, peek-a-boo, and other baby games; reading to baby, rocking to sleep, singing to sleep, soothing away tears, and tucking in bed. For extra fun, fill a water table or small tub with water. Wash and dry the babies using baby shampoo and fluffy baby towels. (Note: Dolls must be washable for the bath activity.) Look at pictures of babies and what they do for more ideas.

Topical sings to be learned: baby, bottle, change, sleep, bed, bath, water, wash, clothes, eat, spoon, bowl, book, sing, toys.
Indicators: A.1.a, A.1.b, A.1.c, A.1.d, A.2.a, A.2.b, A.2.c, B.1.c, B.2.a, B.2.b, B.2.c, C.2.b, E.3.a, F.1.b, F.2.a, F.2.b, F.2.c, F.2.d, F.2.e, F.2.f, F.2.g, F.3.a, F.3.b, F.3.c, F.4.b, F.4.c, F.5.a, G.1.a, G.1.b, G.2.a, G.3.a, H.1.a, H.1.b, H.1.d, H.2.a.

Dramatic Play: Birthday (holidays)

Materials: table and chairs, play-dough, birthday candles, crayons, glue, markers, paper, scissors, tape, crepe paper, balloons, boxes, wrapping paper, card stock, old birthday cards, dress-up clothes, gift bags or fancy boxes, ribbons and bows, party favors and prizes, party plates, napkins, cups, plastic silverware, tablecloth.

Celebrate the birthday (or unbirthday) of a friend, family member, pet, or favorite toy. Make invitations with paper and markers, if desired. Set up a table and chairs. Decorate the room with crepe paper and balloons, if desired. Make a cake out of play-dough with real candles stuck into it. Decorate the cake with any collage items to make it pretty. (Do not eat, of course.) Or make or buy a real cake to eat. Enjoy the pretend (or real) cake, and sing/sign "Happy Birthday." You can wrap boxes so the lids come off, so they can be opened

Copyright © 2008 Time to Sign, Inc.

Family, Home, Holidays, & Transportation

again. It's fun to put small toys or other pretend gifts inside. Create birthday cards on heavy stock paper or construction paper. Old birthday cards can also be cut and pasted to create new designs. Play party games like "Pin the Tail on the Donkey."

Topical signs to be learned: birthday, party, cake, candle, decorate, crayons, paper, scissors, balloon, games, plate, napkin, spoon, fork, knife.
Indicators: A.1.a, A.1.b, A.1.c, A.1.d, A.2.a, A.2.b, A.2.c, B.1.c, B.2.a, B.2.b, B.2.c, C.2.b, E.3.a, F.1.a, F.1.b, F.2.a, F.2.b, F.2.c, F.2.d, F.2.e, F.2.f, F.2.g, F.3.a, F.3.b, F.3.c, F.4.b, F.4.c, G.1.a, G.1.b, G.2.a, G.3.a, H.1.a, H.1.b, H.1.d, H.2.a.

Dramatic Play: Daylight Pajama Party (home, friends)

Materials: "Goodnight Moon" by Margaret Wise Brown, pajamas, blanket or sleeping bag, pillow, stuffed animal, bedtime snack (example: cookies and milk), optional props like those things found in the little bunny's room such as a bedside lamp, dollhouse, mouse etc.

Read the book "Goodnight Moon." Notice all the things the mother bunny in the rocking chair helps the little bunny say goodnight to in his great green room. After reading the book, set up a cozy pretend bed made of a blanket or sleeping bag and pillow. Bring a favorite stuffed toy. Keep it simple with just a few props or add many props. Wear pajamas and snuggle into the pretend bed. Have a bedtime snack. Say goodnight to everything in the room, just like the bunny in the story. Then pretend to go to sleep. Maybe take a real nap!

More Ideas: Bake sugar cookies that look like moons and stars. Play with doll furniture set up like a bedroom , with a toy baby bunny in the bed, and a mama bunny in the rocking chair. Reenact the story through play. A flannel board is also a good way to reenact the story.

Topic Signs to learn: goodnight, signs from "Goodnight Moon," toy, bed, pillow, pretend, snack, sleep, cookies, milk, play.
Indicators: A.1.a, A.1.b, A.1.c, A.1.d, A.2.a, A.2.b, A.2.c, B.1.c, B.2.a, B.2.b, B.2.c, C.2.b, E.3.a, F.1.a, F.1.b, F.2.a, F.2.b, F.2.c, F.2.d, F.2.e, F.2.f, F.2.g, F.3.a, F.3.b, F.3.c, F.4.b, F.4.c, F.5.a, G.1.a, G.1.b, G.2.a, G.3.a, H.1.a, H.1.b, H.1.d, H.2.a.

Dreidel (Hanukkah)

Materials: dreidels, tokens-rains, nuts, toothpicks, pennies, etc.; bowl (pot).

To play Dreidel, each player puts one token into the pot. One player spins the dreidel. If the dreidel lands on "N," the player receives nothing. If it lands on "G," the player receives all the tokens in the pot. If it lands on "H," the player gets half. If it lands on "S," the player adds two tokens to the pot. The game continues until one player has won all the tokens.
Topical signs to be learned: dreidel (top), bowl, game, play, N, G, H, S, all, half, nothing, two.
Indicators: A.1.a, A.1.b, A.1.c, A.1.d, A.2.a, A.2.b, A.2.c, B.1.c, B.2.a, B.2.b, B.2.c, C.2.b, F.1.b, F.2.b, F.2.c, F.2.e, F.2.h, F.3.a, F.3.c, F.4.a, G.1.a, G.1.b, G.2.a, H.1.a, H.1.b, H.1.c, H.1.d.

Easter Egg Hunt (holidays)

Put appropriate goodies or snacks into plastic Easter Eggs. Hide them on the playground or around the classroom. Let the children hunt for them. Keep a couple of extra eggs with you in case a child does not find any, then help them to find some of your extras. After everyone is done have the children sit in a circle. Have them take turns signing the colors of their

Copyright © 2008 Time to Sign, Inc.

eggs and help them to count in sign how many they received. To insure fairness you can write the children's names on the eggs and then they are only to pick up those with their names.

Topical signs to be learned: Easter, egg, basket, snack, candy, hide, find, sit in circle, color signs, number signs, count, write, names.
Indicators: A.1.a, A.1.b, A.1.c, A.1.d, A.2.a, A.2.b, A.2.c, B.1.c, B.2.a, B.2.b, B.2.c, C.2.b, F.1.b, F.2.b, F.2.c, F.2.e, F.2.h, F.3.a, F.3.c, F.4.a, G.1.a, G.1.b, G.2.a, G.3.a, H.1.d, H.2.a.

Family Book (family)
Materials: newsprint, construction paper, stapler, markers/crayons/pencils. Books can be made using newsprint and construction paper

Each child is given a book at the beginning of the unit with a caption on each page such as, "My mother is special because...", "My dad can...", "Grandparents are special because...", "The best part of being a brother/sister is...". Each day the children are asked to draw a different picture and complete the sentence with your help. This then makes a wonderful book to bring home and 'read'.

Topical signs to be learned: book, read, family signs, special, can, best, draw, picture, bring, home, etc.
Indicators: A.1.a, A.1.b, A.1.c, A.1.d, A.2.a, A.2.b, A.2.c, B.1.c, B.2.a, B.2.b, B.2.c, B.3.a, B.3.b, B.4.a, B.5.a, B.5.b, B.5.c, C.2.b, F.1.b, F.2.b, F.2.c, F.2.e, F.2.h, F.3.a, F.3.c, F.4.a, F.5.a, G.1.a, G.1.b, G.2.a, H.1.c, H.1.d

Family Display (family)
Materials: large green paper for the cut-out tree, fingerpaints, children's family pictures, pain brushes and smocks.

Hang a large tree that the children can help create by finger-painting the top and painting the trunk with paintbrushes. Place pictures of the children's families all over the tree. Family pictures can include anyone and be of whomever the children and individual families consider a part of their family.

Topical signs to be learned: tree, paint, family signs, picture.
Indicators: A.1.b, A.1.c, A.1.d, A.2.a, A.2.b, A.2.c, B.1.c, C.2.b, F.1.b, F.2.b, F.2.c, F.2.d, F.2.e, F.2.h, F.3.c, G.1.a, G.1.b, G.2.a, H.1.a, H.1.b, H.1.c, H.1.d.

Grandparent's Day (family)
Have a grandparent's day party, or invite a different grandparent each day to read a special story. Be sure that stories are well rehearsed, and interesting to the children.
Talk about members in a family, father, mother, sister, brother, grandparents, aunts, uncles, cousins, and more.

Topical signs to be learned: family signs, read, story, special.
Indicators: A.1.a, A.1.b, A.1.c, A.1.d, A.2.a, A.2.b, A.2.c, B.1.c, B.2.a, B.2.b, B.2.c, C.2.b, F.1.b, F.2.b, F.2.c, F.2.e, F.2.h, F.3.a, F.3.c, F.4.a, F.5.a, G.1.a, G.1.b, G.2.a, H.1.d, H.2.a.

Family, Home, Holidays, & Transportation

Greeting Card Puzzles (holidays)
Materials: old greeting cards, scissors, small plastic bags.

Cut the fronts of old greeting cards into puzzle pieces or have children cut them into puzzle pieces. Place the pieces to each card in separate plastic bags. Children put puzzles together. You can make one for each child to bring home to use.

Topical signs to be used: puzzle, scissors.
Indicators: A.1.a, A.1.b, A.1.c, A.1.d, A.2.a, A.2.b, A.2.c, B.1.c, B.2.a, B.2.b, B.2.c, C.2.b, F.1.b, F.2.b, F.2.c, F.2.e, F.2.h, F.3.a, F.3.c, F.4.a, G.1.a, G.1.b, G.2.a, H.1.c, H.1.d

Holiday Bingo (holidays)
Have the children create their own bingo boards by choosing where to place different holiday items and glue them into place. Teach them the signs for the different items on their bingo cards. They can also color, cut and paste them onto the bingo card depending on age/ability. December Seasonal items include: dreidel, menorah, stocking, snow flake, snow man, wreath, ornaments, angel, Kwanzaa cloth, basket, muhindi, candle, reindeer, sleigh, etc. This game can be altered by choosing different items for different holidays.

Topical signs to be learned: holiday signs, holiday items signs.
Indicators: A.1.a, A.1.b, A.1.c, A.1.d, A.2.a, A.2.b, A.2.c, B.1.c, B.2.a, B.2.b, B.2.c, C.2.b, F.1.b, F.2.b, F.2.c, F.2.e, F.2.h, F.3.a, F.3.c, F.4.a, F.5.a, G.1.a, G.1.b, G.2.a, G.3.a, H.1.c, H.1.d

How far will the car go? (transportation)
Materials: toy car, yarn or rulers and yardsticks.

Have the children examine the toy car. Ask for predictions of whether the car would roll the farthest on a bare surface, on a rug, or on cement. Have the children roll the car on different surfaces and measure with the yarn the distance the car traveled. You can also use rules and yardsticks to measure the distance. Talk about which surface the car traveled the farthest. Talk about how the surfaces are the same or different. Talk about types of roads and surfaces that are easy and hard to drive/skate/ride a bike on.

Topical signs to be learned: car, go, far, smooth, hard, measure, same, different, road/street.
Indicators: A.1.a, A.1.b, A.1.c, A.1.d, A.2.a, A.2.b, A.2.c, B.1.c, B.2.a, B.2.b, B.2.c, C.2.b, F.1.b, F.2.b, F.2.c, F.2.d, F.2.e, F.2.h, F.3.a, F.3.c, F.4.a, G.1.a, G.1.b, G.2.a, G.3.a, H.1.a, H.1.d, H.2.a.

"I Love My Family Because..." (family)
Materials: paper, pen/marker.

Have the children complete the sentence "I Love My Family Because..." Write down the children's answers and post them on a bulletin board.

Topical signs to be learned: I, love, my, family, because, write, why.
Indicators: A.1.a, A.1.b, A.1.c, A.1.d, A.2.a, A.2.b, A.2.c, B.1.c, B.2.a, B.2.b, B.2.c, B.3.a, B.3.b, B.4.a, B.5.a, B.5.b, B.5.c, C.2.b, F.1.b, F.2.a, F.2.b, F.2.c, F.2.e, F.2.h, F.3.a, F.3.c, F.4.a, F.5.a, G.1.a, G.1.b, G.2.a, H.1.c, H.1.d.

Family, Home, Holidays, & Transportation

Letter to Santa (holidays)
Materials: paper, pencils.

Have the children write a letter to Santa. Take it to the mall or other place that accepts these letters.

Topical signs to be learned: paper, pencil, letter, write, Christmas, want, toy, mail.
Indicators: A.1.a, A.1.b, A.1.c, A.1.d, A.2.a, A.2.b, A.2.c, B.1.c, B.2.a, B.2.b, B.2.c, B.3.a, B.3.b, B.4.a, B.5.a, B.5.b, B.5.c, C.2.b, F.1.b, F.2.a, F.2.b, F.2.c, F.2.e, F.2.h, F.3.a, F.3.c, F.4.a, F.5.a, G.1.a, G.1.b, G.2.a, H.1.c, H.1.d.

Mother May I? (family, manners)
Have children stand behind a line, real or imaginary, and one person be "mother" and stand a ways away from the rest of the group. The "Mother" tells each person one by one how many and what type of steps they can take. For example, "take three baby/little steps" (giant/big, ant/tiny, ballerina, hop, etc). The child has to say and sign "mother may I" and the "mother" replies "yes, you may." If they do not ask "mother may I" and proceed to take their steps then they must go back to the starting line. The first person to reach the "mother" becomes the new "mother."
Replace mother with other family members.

Topical signs to be learned: family signs, may (can), I, yes, you, take, number signs, walk, go, line, start, big, little, tiny, jump.
Indicators: A.1.a, A.1.b, A.1.c, A.1.d, A.2.a, A.2.b, A.2.c, B.1.c, B.2.a, B.2.b, B.2.c, C.2.b, F.1.b, F.2.b, F.2.c, F.2.e, F.2.f, F.2.h, F.3.a, F.3.c, F.4.a, G.1.a, G.1.b, G.2.a, G.3.a, H.1.d, H.2.a.

My Ship is Loaded (transportation)
Materials: one ball per group

Have the group sit in a circle formation. One person starts the activity by rolling the ball to another student, saying and signing "My ship is loaded with bananas" (or any other cargo he or she wishes) Sign: my + boat + have...). The second player receiving the ball has to repeat what the first student said and signed and add another item to the list. "My ship is loaded with bananas and cups." She then rolls the ball to another player. Each player who receives the ball has to repeat what the other players have said and add another item. When a player fails to repeat all the cargo, the ball is given to the player on their right as the game continues. This activity can be played with the entire group sitting in a large circle, or you can divide them into smaller groups. Besides encouraging group interaction, this game can also be used to help everyone learn the names and name signs of the others in the group. Instead of saying an object, the first person says their name and signs their name sign. The other students that receive the ball must repeat all the names and name signs given.

Topical signs to be learned: ball, roll, sit in circle, my, ship/boat, add, name, name signs.
Indicators: A.1.a, A.1.b, A.1.c, A.1.d, A.2.a, A.2.b, A.2.c, B.1.c, B.2.a, B.2.b, B.2.c, C.2.b, F.1.a, F.1.b, F.2.b, F.2.c, F.2.e, F.2.h, F.3.a, F.3.c, F.4.a, F.5.a, G.1.a, G.1.b, G.2.a, G.3.a, H.1.c, H.1.d

Family, Home, Holidays, & Transportation

New Year's Parade (holidays, New Year's)
Materials: construction paper, yarn, hole punch, glue, paper scraps, ribbon, tinsel glitter, other materials as desired to decorate, rhythm instruments, music.

Make small cone-shaped hats out of construction paper and attach yarn to the side for ties. Have children decorate their hats. When dry, help children put on hats and give each a rhythm instrument. Play music and let them march around the room in a New Year's Parade.

Topical signs to be learned: New Year's, hat, march, music.
Indicators: A.1.a, A.1.b, A.1.c, A.1.d, A.2.a, A.2.b, A.2.c, B.1.c, B.2.a, B.2.b, B.2.c, C.2.b, E.1.a, E.3.a, F.1.b, F.2.a, F.2.b, F.2.c, F.2.d, F.2.e, F.2.h, F.3.a, F.3.b, F.3.c, F.4.b, G.1.a, G.1.b, G.2.a, H.1.a, H.1.b, H.1.d, H.2.a.

Pull the Sled (transportation)
Have the children work with partners. One child will pull the sled; the other will be the sled in the snow. The "sled" puts his or her hands on the puller's waist to represent a rope. The puller drags the sled through the snow until they come to a hill. They have trouble getting up the hill. When they reach the top of the hill, the puller moves behind the sled, and the sled runs quickly down the hill.

Topical signs to be learned: sled, snow, run, up, down, hill (mountain).
Indicators: A.1.a, A.1.b, A.1.c, A.1.d, A.2.a, A.2.b, A.2.c, B.1.c, B.2.a, B.2.b, B.2.c, C.2.b, F.1.b, F.2.b, F.2.c, F.2.e, F.2.h, F.3.a, F.3.c, F.4.b, G.1.a, G.1.b, G.2.a, H.1.d, H.2.a.

Railroad Train (transportation)
Materials: cardboard boxes (at least 2 feet long), paper punch, paper tickets, triangle or bell, whistle, shakers or maracas, books on trains.

Share a book or books about trains with the children. Line cardboard boxes up behind each other, the front is the engine and the rest are passenger cars. One child can play engineer, one can be given a triangle or bell to signal the start of the train, another can make wheel sounds and so on. Pieces of paper can be distributed as tickets and then collected by a conductor (These can be made by the children before this activity).

Topical signs to be learned: train, book, ride, sit, ticket, give.
Indicators: A.1.a, A.1.b, A.1.c, A.1.d, A.2.a, A.2.b, A.2.c, B.1.c, B.2.a, B.2.b, B.2.c, C.2.b, F.1.b, F.2.b, F.2.c, F.2.e, F.2.h, F.3.a, F.3.c, F.4.b, G.1.a, G.1.b, G.2.a, H.1.d, H.2.a.

Red Light, Green Light (transportation)
One player stands on an imaginary line and is It. The rest of the players in a straight line some distance away, each trying to be the first to cross the finish line and win. It turns their back to the players and yells "Green Light!" At this signal all the players hurry toward the finish line. But as soon as It yells "Red light!" and spins around to face the other players, they must all freeze. Anyone It catches moving is sent back to the starting line. The first player to cross the finish line wins and becomes It for the next game.

Topical signs to be learned: cross, line, hurry, freeze, catch, light, red, green, start, stop, go, line, finish, win, spin.

Copyright © 2008 Time to Sign, Inc.

Family, Home, Holidays, & Transportation

Indicators: A.1.a, A.1.b, A.1.c, A.1.d, A.2.a, A.2.b, A.2.c, B.1.c, B.2.a, B.2.b, B.2.c, C.2.b, F.1.b, F.2.b, F.2.c, F.2.e, F.2.h, F.3.a, F.3.c, F.4.b, G.1.a, G.1.b, G.2.a, H.1.d, H.2.a.

Rocket Ship Trip (transportation)
Materials: paper rockets or rocket toys, jar of marbles.

Bring all the rocket ships to an area such as a rug and stand them up. This is earth. Talk about rocket ships (their uses, who uses them, why, etc.).
Take a trip to the moon. Pass the jar of marbles around. Each child gives it a few strong shakes to start their rocket engine. Now count down from ten to one. When you get to one, everyone says, "Blast off!" Slowly move the rocket ships from earth around the room. Move silently. Space is very quiet. Say "I see the moon" and slowly head towards the paper moon on the wall. When the rockets have passed the moon, head back to earth and slowly land the ships.

Topical signs to be learned: rocket, earth, moon, star, astronaut, travel, numbers 1-10, quiet, see.
Indicators: A.1.b, A.1.c, A.1.d, A.2.a, A.2.b, A.2.c, B.1.c, C.1.a, C.1.b, C.1.d, C.2.b, F.1.b, F.2.b, F.2.c, F.2.d, F.2.e, F.2.h, F.3.c, G.1.a, G.1.b, G.2.a, H.1.b, H.1.d.

Seasonal Transportation (weather, transportation)
Materials: magazines, catalogs or pictures printed from the internet, scissors, glue, poster board or construction paper.

Cut out pictures of seasonal transportation (snowplows, sleds, skis, snow mobiles, snow shoes, row boats, sailboats, RVs, convertibles, hot-air balloons, trucks, motorcycles, bicycles, tricycles, skateboards, roller skates, horses). Mount the pictures on construction paper or poster board.
Discuss the word "transportation." Show the pictures of different transportation and have children identify them. Show the signs for the different types of transportation (or have children show you the signs if they already know them). Ask what type of weather is best for each vehicle and use weather signs. Ask them what would happen if we traveled on a sled on skis on a hot, sunny day or in a row boat on a rainy day, etc. Then have the children pick one way of traveling and take an imaginary trip on a snowy, rainy, sunny, or windy day. You can also have pictures of different types of weather and have children match the transportation pictures with the weather pictures.

Topical signs to be learned: transportation signs, weather signs, picture.
Indicators: A.1.a, A.1.b, A.1.c, A.1.d, A.2.a, A.2.b, A.2.c, B.1.c, B.2.a, B.2.b, B.2.c, C.2.b, D.1.b, D.2.b, D.2.c, D.2.d, F.1.a, F.1.b, F.2.b, F.2.c, F.2.e, F.2.h, F.3.a, F.3.c, F.4.a, G.1.a, G.1.b, G.2.a, G.3.a, H.1.a, H.1.d.

Teddy Bear Games (home, math)
Materials: large group of teddy bears.

Let children count the total number of teddy bears. Have the children sort the teddy bears by categories (color, size, ones with bows, etc.). Then have them count the number of bears in each category. This information can be recorded on a chalkboard or chart paper. Have

Family, Home, Holidays, & Transportation

the children make different sets of teddy bears (3 black bears, 2 white, etc.). Have children compare the weight of two different bears by holding one in each hand and ask them which feels heavier and which feels lighter.

Topical signs to be learned: teddy bear, count, number signs, heavy, light (weight), color signs, separate/divide.
Indicators: A.1.a, A.1.b, A.1.c, A.1.d, A.2.a, A.2.b, A.2.c, B.1.c, B.2.a, B.2.b, B.2.c, C.1.a, C.1.b, C.1.d., C.2.b, F.1.b, F.2.b, F.2.c, F.2.d, F.2.e, F.2.h, F.3.a, F.3.c, F.4.a, G.1.a, G.1.b, G.2.a, G.3.a, H.1.d, H.2.a.

Traffic Course (transportation)

Materials: riding toys, playground or indoor gym, carpet sample scraps, chalk, masking tape, ropes, string, washable paint (for making roads and streets); cardboard boxes, chairs, coat racks, crayons, heavy paper or newsprint, paint easels, paints, brushes (for making traffic signs); traffic cones, wide markers; clothespins, crepe paper, fabric scraps, flags, newspaper, ribbons, sewing trim, stapler, streamers, tape, yarn (for decorating riding toys); broom dustpan.

Read about cars and trucks for enjoyment. Build an obstacle or traffic course on a playground or large indoor area. Sweep the area clean of rocks glass or debris. Spread out and arrange materials to indicate roads, paths, or streets from the list above. Have cross streets, one way streets, and speedways. Next put up signs made from boxes, posted on chairs or easels, or sticking on traffic cones. Begin with two or three signs and add others as needed. Signs to make are Bridge Ahead, Carpool Lane, Do Not Enter, Exit Only, Gas Ahead, Left Turn Only, One Way, Park, Speed Limit __mph, Stop, Yield. Drive riding toys through the traffic plan, paying attention to signs and rules. You can have a police officer who gives tickets to those violating the traffic rules. As a culmination, decorate the vehicles and have a parade through the course, with all traffic except the main street blocked off, of course. Play parade music if desired.

Topical signs to be learned: transportation vehicle signs, chalk, crayon, chair, paper, paint, flag, road/street, traffic, traffic light, stop, police officer, ticket, bridge, parade, music.
Indicators: A.1.a, A.1.b, A.1.c, A.1.d, A.2.a, A.2.b, A.2.c, B.1.c, B.2.a, B.2.b, B.2.c, C.2.b, F.1.b, F.2.b, F.2.c, F.2.e, F.2.h, F.3.a, F.3.c, F.4.b, G.1.a, G.1.b, G.2.a, H.1.d, H.2.a.

Traffic Light (trans.)

Explain what each color means, sing "Traffic Light" song and then teach a few other traffic signs (slow down, stop, go).

Topical signs to be learned: traffic light, red, yellow, green, stop, slow, go, fast.
Indicators: A.1.a, A.1.b, A.1.c, A.1.d, A.2.a, A.2.b, A.2.c, B.1.c, B.2.a, B.2.b, B.2.c, C.2.b, F.1.b, F.2.b, F.2.c, F.2.e, F.2.h, F.3.a, F.3.c, F.4.b, G.1.a, G.1.b, G.2.a, H.1.b, H.1.d.

Train Sequence (transportation, math)

Materials: construction paper train cars, construction paper engine and caboose, sticky dots or marker.

Place dots or numbers on train cars. The children arrange the cars from smallest number or number of dots to largest number or number of dots.

Copyright © 2008 Time to Sign, Inc.

Family, Home, Holidays, & Transportation

Topical signs to be learned: train, caboose, number signs.
Indicators: A.1.a, A.1.b, A.1.c, A.1.d, A.2.a, A.2.b, A.2.c, B.1.c, B.2.a, B.2.b, B.2.c, B.3.a, C.1.a, C.1.b, C.1.d., C.2.b, F.1.b, F.2.b, F.2.c, F.2.d, F.2.e, F.2.h, F.3.a, F.3.c, F.4.a, G.1.a, G.1.b, G.2.a, G.3.a, H.1.b, H.1.d.

Trucking Shapes (transportation, shapes)
Materials: construction paper, poster board, glue.

Make a truck out of construction paper for each shape you are doing. Glue the truck shape to a piece of poster board but do not glue the top strip of the truck bed, leaving a pocket for the shapes. Glue a different shape to the bed of each truck. Help the children trace or draw and color different shapes. Encourage the children to match their shapes to the right shape on a truck and put their shape into the right truck.

Topical signs to be learned: shape signs, same, different.
Indicators: A.1.a, A.1.b, A.1.c, A.1.d, A.2.a, A.2.b, A.2.c, B.1.c, B.2.a, B.2.b, B.2.c, C.2.a, C.2.b, F.1.b, F.2.b, F.2.c, F.2.d, F.2.e, F.2.h, F.3.a, F.3.c, F.4.a, G.1.a, G.1.b, G.2.a, G.3.a, H.1.d, H.2.a.

Vacations (transportation)
Materials: paper, pen, pencil or markers.

Discussion. Send home a note asking parents to send in a picture from their family vacation. Display pictures on wall under caption ***"Summer Fun"***. Have children tell you something special about their vacation. Write and post the sentence under their picture. Talk about different vacations the children experienced.

Topical signs to be learned: send, home, picture, family, summer, fun, tell, special, write.
Indicators: A.1.a, A.1.b, A.1.c, A.1.d, A.2.a, A.2.b, A.2.c, B.1.c, B.2.a, B.2.b, B.2.c, B.3.a, B.3.b, B.4.a, B.5.a, B.5.b, B.5.c, C.2.b, F.1.b, F.2.a, F.2.b, F.2.c, F.2.e, F.2.h, F.3.a, F.3.c, F.4.a, F.5.a, G.1.a, G.1.b, G.2.a, H.1.c, H.1.d.

Weather and Homes (weather, home)
Materials: magazines or catalogs, scissors, glue, construction paper or poster board, index cards.

Cut out pictures of various homes such as an apartment, house, trailer, tent, bungalow, beach house, camper, ski lodge, igloo, hut, etc. Glue them onto construction paper or poster board. Complete a scene for winter, spring, summer, and fall, and glue the pictures on index cards.

Have the children name each home. Then have the children identify seasonal scenes. Discuss how some homes and buildings are built for specific weather or seasons. Ask the children to pick homes that would be best for each season and discuss the reasons why. You can also give the pictures to the children and have them match the homes with the seasons.

Topical signs to be learned: season signs, house, home, weather signs.
Indicators: A.1.a, A.1.b, A.1.c, A.1.d, A.2.a, A.2.b, A.2.c, B.1.c, B.2.a, B.2.b, B.2.c, C.2.b, D.1.b, D.2.b, D.2.c, D.2.d, F.1.a, F.1.b, F.2.b, F.2.c, F.2.e, F.2.h, F.3.a, F.3.c, F.4.a, G.1.a, G.1.b, G.2.a, G.3.a, H.1.a, H.1.d.

Copyright © 2008 Time to Sign, Inc.

Family, Home, Holidays, & Transportation

Where's Santa?" (holidays)
Materials: stuffed Santa or felt Santa, flannel board, felt pieces depicting classroom items and holiday items.

Using a stuffed Santa, hide Santa in various places around the room. Sign to the class "Where's Santa?" Have children look and find Santa. Can also be done using flannel board patterns, "hide" Santa in various places. Sign "Where's Santa?" and have children sign where he is.

Topical signs to be learned: Santa (show the outline of a beard from the chin with the claw hand), where, look for, find.
Indicators: A.1.a, A.1.b, A.1.c, A.1.d, A.2.a, A.2.b, A.2.c, B.1.c, B.2.a, B.2.b, B.2.c, B.3.a, C.1.a, C.1.b, C.1.d., C.2.b, F.1.b, F.2.b, F.2.c, F.2.d, F.2.e, F.2.h, F.3.a, F.3.c, F.4.a, G.1.a, G.1.b, G.2.a, G.3.a, H.1.b, H.1.d, H.2.a.

Crafts

Angel Pattern (holidays)
Materials: Copy paper, construction paper, scissors (if old enough), glue sticks, paper cut outs and crayons.

Have the children color and decorate an angel (older children may cut out themselves).

Topical signs to be learned: angel, white, wings, dress.
Indicators: A.1.b, A.1.c, A.1.d, A.2.a, A.2.b, A.2.c, B.1.c, C.2.b, F.1.b, F.2.b, F.2.c, F.2.d, F.2.e, F.2.h, F.3.c, G.1.a, G.1.b, G.2.a, H.1.a, H.1.b, H.1.c, H.1.d.

Barges (transportation)
Materials: several clean Styrofoam meat trays, hole punch, and yarn.

Punch a hole in opposite ends of each of several foam meat trays. Connect the trays with yarn to make a barge.

Topical signs to be learned: boat, string.
Indicators: A.1.b, A.1.c, A.1.d, A.2.a, A.2.b, A.2.c, B.1.c, C.2.b, F.1.b, F.2.b, F.2.c, F.2.d, F.2.e, F.2.h, F.3.c, G.1.a, G.1.b, G.2.a, H.1.a, H.1.b, H.1.c, H.1.d.

Box Train (transportation)
Materials: shoe boxes, cardboard, scissors, glue, heavy string, pencil, brass paper fasteners, spools, small bell, cardboard tubes, oatmeal or salt box, tempera paint and paint brushes(optional).

Engine: To make a shoe-box engine, find two boxes, one just enough smaller to fit snugly inside the other. For the cab, cut away about 1/3 of the smaller box. Cut holes in the sides for windows. Insert the larger section of the smaller box upright in the bigger box, with open sides facing back. Attach a brass fastener in front of the large box for a headlight. Use drinking glasses for patterns, cut six disks from cardboard and attach with brass paper fasteners for wheels. No measure the depth of the cab box and cut away this amount from the large box lid. Glue or tape the lid to its own box, in front of the cab. Glue two spools into

Copyright © 2008 Time to Sign, Inc.

position for smokestacks. Glue or tie together two matchsticks or use a small stick and tie on a small bell. This engine is large enough to carry men, dolls, or animals, If wheels are not fastened too tightly, they will roll.

Box Cars: Use boxes with lids for box cars. Cut doors in the sides large enough to insert toys. To hold door shut, use brass fasteners on the doors far enough apart to be held with a rubber band.

Gondolas: Use a lidless box. Cut out and attach cardboard wheels with brass fasteners.

Flat Cars: The lids left over from the gondolas can be used. Cut out and attach wheels with brass fasteners.

Tankers: Use oatmeal or salt boxes glued to show box lids. Cut out cardboard wheels and fasten with brass fasteners.

Tie cars and engine together with heavy string. To permit uncoupling, punch a small hole for the string. Cut a narrow slit from this hole up to another large enough hole to permit knot to slip through. To add more realism these can be painted with poster paints, but this should be done before assembling. Paint different names, symbols, and slogans on the sides, similar to those on real trains.

Topical signs to be learned: train, shoe box, wheels, scissors, glue, paint, windows, measure, bell, door, string.
Indicators: A.1.b, A.1.c, A.1.d, A.2.a, A.2.b, A.2.c, B.1.c, C.2.b, F.1.b, F.2.b, F.2.c, F.2.d, F.2.e, F.2.h, F.3.c, G.1.a, G.1.b, G.2.a, H.1.a, H.1.b, H.1.c, H.1.d.

Boats (transportation)
Walnut Boat
Materials: walnut shell or split peach stone, toothpick, paper, scissors, glue or clay.

Push a one-inch length of toothpick through a tiny triangle of paper for a sail. Drop a blob of glue into the walnut shell or peach stone and prop the sail in this until set, or use a very tiny ball of clay stuck fast.

Bottle-Cap Boat
Materials: Bottle cap or milk cap, toothpick, paper.

Push a one-inch length of toothpick through a tiny triangle of paper for a sail. Attach this to the cork inside a soft-drink bottle cap or a waxed milk cap.

Box Boat
Materials: cream or milk cartons of any size, scissors, foil or paint and brushes.

Press in the pouring spout and cut out one side of cream or milk carton. Push one end out slightly to form a prow. Glue foil to the sides to cover advertising or paint.

Family, Home, Holidays, & Transportation

Bark Boat
Materials: chunks of bark in varying sizes from 3-4 inches long to as big as you can handle (Pin bark (mulch) is available at garden shops), sticks, leaves, an oyster shucker/awl/ice pick, small cup hooks and string (optional).

Bore a small hole in the center of the piece of bark to hold the mast for the sail. If you have a very large piece of bark, you may want to have more than one mast. Have the children bore the holes. Depending on the sharpness of the tools they're using, they will need more or less supervision. Thread a large leaf onto a stick, and place the stick in the hole. If you want to attach string so the children can pull their boats (or not lose them downstream!), screw a small cup hook into the front edge and tie on a string.

Sail the boats in a big tub of water or water table or, better yet, take the children to a creek or stream and really let them sail!

Topical signs to be learned: boat, sailboat, sailing, paper, scissors, triangle, glue, paint, leaves.
Indicators: A.1.b, A.1.c, A.1.d, A.2.a, A.2.b, A.2.c, B.1.c, C.2.b, F.1.b, F.2.b, F.2.c, F.2.d, F.2.e, F.2.h, F.3.c, G.1.a, G.1.b, G.2.a, H.1.a, H.1.b, H.1.c, H.1.d.

Bunnies (pets, holidays)
Materials: pre-drawn rabbit pattern, cotton balls, glue or glue sticks, brown or white paint (if painting) and paint brushes, and smocks.

Paint pre-cut bunny shapes, if desired. Glue cotton balls onto a pre-cut bunny shape. Talk about the soft texture of a bunny.

Topical signs to be learned: bunny/rabbit, white, brown, glue, paint, soft, feel.
Indicators: A.1.b, A.1.c, A.1.d, A.2.a, A.2.b, A.2.c, B.1.c, C.2.b, F.1.b, F.2.b, F.2.c, F.2.d, F.2.e, F.2.h, F.3.c, G.1.a, G.1.b, G.2.a, H.1.a, H.1.b, H.1.c, H.1.d.

Candles (holidays)
Materials: Copy paper, construction paper, scissors (if old enough), glue sticks, paper cut outs and crayons.

Have the children color and decorate a candle (older children may make the cut outs themselves). The cut out decorations should include a flame and a base.

Topical signs to be learned: candle, light, hot.
Indicators: A.1.b, A.1.c, A.1.d, A.2.a, A.2.b, A.2.c, B.1.c, C.2.b, F.1.b, F.2.b, F.2.c, F.2.d, F.2.e, F.2.h, F.3.c, G.1.a, G.1.b, G.2.a, H.1.a, H.1.b, H.1.c, H.1.d.

Candles II (holidays)
Materials: pre-cut candlesticks, oaktag squares, fingerpaint (red, yellow and orange) and smocks.

Have children finger paint flames to attach to pre-cut candlesticks.

Copyright © 2008 Time to Sign, Inc.

Family, Home, Holidays, & Transportation

Topical signs to be learned: candle, light, hot, paint, red, yellow, orange.
Indicators: A.1.b, A.1.c, A.1.d, A.2.a, A.2.b, A.2.c, B.1.c, C.2.b, F.1.b, F.2.b, F.2.c, F.2.d, F.2.e, F.2.h, F.3.c, G.1.a, G.1.b, G.2.a, H.1.a, H.1.b, H.1.c, H.1.d.

Christmas Tree Lights (holidays)
Materials: green construction paper, scissors, glue, red/yellow/blue tempera paint, cotton swabs.

Cut out Christmas tree shapes from the paper. Mix a few tablespoons of glue with each paint color. Have the children dip the cotton swabs in the colored glue and make dots on the trees.
Topical signs to be learned: Christmas, tree, light, red, yellow, blue, paint, glue.
Indicators: A.1.b, A.1.c, A.1.d, A.2.a, A.2.b, A.2.c, B.1.c, C.2.b, F.1.b, F.2.b, F.2.c, F.2.d, F.2.e, F.2.h, F.3.c, G.1.a, G.1.b, G.2.a, H.1.a, H.1.b, H.1.c, H.1.d.

Colorful Clay Ornaments (holidays)
Materials: ¾ cup flour, ½ cup cornmeal, ½ cup salt, hot water, food coloring, waxed paper, small plastic sandwich bags, large bowl, measuring cups, wooden spoon, newspaper, rolling pin or large can, cookie cutters, paper clips, poster paint, brushes, white glue, glitter, sequins, clear acrylic paint, ornament hooks, string or leather thong.

In a large bowl, mix together the flour, cornmeal, and salt. With a wooden spoon, stir in ¼ cup of hot tap water. Continue adding water a little at a time until the mixture looks like stiff cookie dough. Do not add too much water—dry clay works better than wet. Divide the clay into two or three batches and put each batch on a piece of waxed paper. Make a hole in the center of each batch and add a few drops of food coloring. Roll the clay and knead it to spread the food coloring evenly. Wear small plastic sandwich bags on your hands while you knead the clay to keep the food coloring from staining your hands.

Cover your work area with newspaper. Sandwich each batch of clay between two pieces of waxed paper. Using a rolling pin or a large can, roll the clay out between the waxed paper until it is ¼ to ½ inch thick. Remove the top piece of waxed paper and cut out shapes with cookie cutters. If you are making ornaments for your room, use cookie cutters of action figures and toys. For Christmas ornaments, use cookie cutters in holiday shapes. Push a partially opened paper clip gently into the top of each shape for a hanging loop. Let the clay shapes dry for 1 to 2 hours, or until they are dry to the touch. Decorate them with poster paint, or glue glitter, sequins, or other decorations onto them. Let the ornaments dry completely (it might take about 2 days), then protect them with a coat of clear acrylic paint. To hang an ornament on the Christmas tree, slip an ornament hook through the paper clip hanging loop. To hang an ornament in your room, thread a piece of string or a narrow leather thong through the top of the paper clip hanging loop.

Topical signs to be learned: salt, hot, water, corn, food coloring, bowl, measure, cup, spoon, paint, glue, string, add, roll, dry.
Indicators: A.1.b, A.1.c, A.1.d, A.2.a, A.2.b, A.2.c, B.1.c, C.2.b, F.1.b, F.2.b, F.2.c, F.2.d, F.2.e, F.2.h, F.3.c, G.1.a, G.1.b, G.2.a, H.1.a, H.1.b, H.1.c, H.1.d.

Cornstarch Clay Ornaments (holidays)
Materials: 3 cups cornstarch, 6 cups baking soda, large pan, 3 ¾ cup water, mixing spoon, dish towel, waxed paper, masking tape, rolling pin or large can, cookie cutters, knife,

Family, Home, Holidays, & Transportation

knitting needle or unsharpened pencil, drying rack, acrylic paint, paint brushes, colored permanent marker, spray shellac or clear acrylic sealer, ribbon or gold cord, glue, photo of child or colored pencil drawing of a Christmas scene.

Combine the cornstarch and baking soda in a large pan. Add the water. Place over low heat. Stir all the while until mixture has the consistency of mashed potatoes. Remove from heat and cover with a moistened dish towel. When the pan is cool enough to handle, remove the clay and knead it until smooth. Cover the working area with waxed paper held down by masking tape. Roll out the clay to ¼" thickness. Cut out shapes using small cookie cutters. Cut out a 1 ½" x 1 ¼" area in the center of each ornament with a knife. Make a centered hole through the top of the ornament using the point of a big knitting needle or an unsharpened pencil. Place the ornaments on a rack to dry overnight. Use acrylic paint thinned with water to paint the ornaments. Allow to dry. Use a bright colored permanent marking pen to print the date or year on the ornament. Give each dried ornament a final coat of spray shellac or clear acrylic sealer. When dry, the ornament is threaded with a short length of ribbon or gold cord through the top hole. Knot the ends of the cord to form a loop. Finally glue a tiny photo of the child or a picture they drew to the back of the ornament (so that it shows through the hole in the center of the ornament).

Topical signs to be learned: bowl, spoon, Christmas, decorate, tree, dry, paint, ribbon, glue, picture, draw.
Indicators: A.1.b, A.1.c, A.1.d, A.2.a, A.2.b, A.2.c, B.1.c, C.2.b, F.1.b, F.2.b, F.2.c, F.2.d, F.2.e, F.2.h, F.3.c, G.1.a, G.1.b, G.2.a, H.1.a, H.1.b, H.1.c, H.1.d.

Egg Carton Train (transportation)
Materials: Cardboard Egg Carton, paint, paint brush, circle stickers, cardboard tubes, and other collage materials.

Give each of your children a row of six egg cups cut lengthwise from a cardboard egg carton. Have the children turn their egg carton sections upside down and paint them to make trains. When the cartons are dry, have the children add details such as round sticker wheels or cardboard-tube smokestacks.

Topical signs to be learned: train, paint, dry, dry, wheels, smoke stack.
Indicators: A.1.b, A.1.c, A.1.d, A.2.a, A.2.b, A.2.c, B.1.c, C.2.b, F.1.b, F.2.b, F.2.c, F.2.d, F.2.e, F.2.h, F.3.c, G.1.a, G.1.b, G.2.a, H.1.a, H.1.b, H.1.c, H.1.d.

Fancy Soaps (holidays, Mother's Day)
Materials: Ivory Snow or soap powder/flakes, water, measuring cup, bowl, food coloring, waxed paper, essential oils or liquid scents (optional); baby food jar, ribbon & stickers (optional); tissue paper & stickers (optional), yarn or string (optional).

These soaps make great Mother's Day or other holiday presents. Tint about ½ cup water desired color. Add a few drops of essential oils if desired for scent. Stir into about 2 cups of soap powder to make a dough-like mixture. Have the children mold the mixture into balls or other shapes or form mixture around a long piece of yarn or string folded in half. Place on waxed paper to dry for several days. If soaps are small, have children put several in a large baby food jar and decorate with stickers and tie a ribbon around the neck of each jar. Or help the children warp their soaps in tissue paper and decorate them with stickers.

Copyright © 2008 Time to Sign, Inc.

Topical signs to be learned: mother's day, give, soap, make, shape signs, dry, decorate.
Indicators: A.1.b, A.1.c, A.1.d, A.2.a, A.2.b, A.2.c, B.1.c, C.2.b, F.1.b, F.2.b, F.2.c, F.2.d, F.2.e, F.2.h, F.3.c, F.5.a, G.1.a, G.1.b, G.2.a, H.1.a, H.1.b, H.1.c, H.1.d.

Fireworks (holidays)
Materials: black construction paper, glue, craft sticks, glitter, and smocks.

Have children use craft sticks to spread lines of glue on black paper. Sprinkle glitter over glue areas. Shake off excess.

Indicators: A.1.b, A.1.c, A.1.d, A.2.a, A.2.b, A.2.c, B.1.c, C.2.b, F.1.b, F.2.b, F.2.c, F.2.d, F.2.e, F.2.h, F.3.c, G.1.a, G.1.b, G.2.a, H.1.a, H.1.b, H.1.c, H.1.d.

Fish (pets)
Materials: pre-cut construction paper fish, glue, and pre-cut tissue paper squares.

Give each child a paper fish. Mix a little glue and a little water in a cup. Give each child a paint brush. They can use this mixture to stick on tissue paper squares.

Topical signs to be learned: fish, color signs, glue, paint, paper.
Indicators: A.1.b, A.1.c, A.1.d, A.2.a, A.2.b, A.2.c, B.1.c, C.2.b, F.1.b, F.2.b, F.2.c, F.2.d, F.2.e, F.2.h, F.3.c, G.1.a, G.1.b, G.2.a, H.1.a, H.1.b, H.1.c, H.1.d.

Fish Tank (pets)
Materials: box, blue paint, glitter, sequins, feathers, and construction paper.

Take a card board box open on one side and have the children paint the inside blue. Then give each child a precut fish (or have them design their own) to decorate with glitter, sequins, feathers, or whatever is on hand. Then suspend the fish with fishing wire from the fish tank. It will look like the fish are swimming. Allow the children to add things to the tank like rocks, plants etc.

Topical signs to be learned: fish, bowl/box, blue, water, rock, plant, pet.
Indicators: A.1.b, A.1.c, A.1.d, A.2.a, A.2.b, A.2.c, B.1.c, C.2.b, F.1.b, F.2.b, F.2.c, F.2.d, F.2.e, F.2.h, F.3.c, G.1.a, G.1.b, G.2.a, H.1.a, H.1.b, H.1.c, H.1.d.

Flag Rainbow Banner (holidays)
Materials: white banner paper, red and blue fingerpaint.

Have the children make a flag rainbow with red and blue handprints on white banner paper.

Indicators: A.1.b, A.1.c, A.1.d, A.2.a, A.2.b, A.2.c, B.1.c, C.2.b, F.1.b, F.2.b, F.2.c, F.2.d, F.2.e, F.2.h, F.3.c, G.1.a, G.1.b, G.2.a, H.1.a, H.1.b, H.1.c, H.1.d.

Fourth of July Banner (holidays)
Materials: white banner paper, red and blue fingerpaints, and markers.

Family, Home, Holidays, & Transportation

Fingerpaint a white banner with red and blue colors. Then the teacher/assistant writes "Happy 4th of July" across the banner. Hang it up where everyone can see it.

Indicators: A.1.b, A.1.c, A.1.d, A.2.a, A.2.b, A.2.c, B.1.c, C.2.b, F.1.b, F.2.b, F.2.c, F.2.d, F.2.e, F.2.h, F.3.c, G.1.a, G.1.b, G.2.a, H.1.a, H.1.b, H.1.c, H.1.d.

Gingerbread Boy or Girl (holidays)

Materials: Copy paper, construction paper, scissors (if old enough), glue sticks, paper cut outs and crayons.
Or
Cookie dough, gingerbread man/woman cookie cutter, icing, sprinkles, and gumdrops.

Have the children decorate a brown paper cut out of a gingerbread boy or girl. Decorations include: cut out eyes, nose, buttons, etc. (older children may cut these out from patterns).
Or
Make gingerbread cookies with icing, sprinkles, and gumdrops for decorations.

Topical signs to be learned: cookie, brown, boy.
Indicators: A.1.b, A.1.c, A.1.d, A.2.a, A.2.b, A.2.c, B.1.c, C.2.b, F.1.b, F.2.b, F.2.c, F.2.d, F.2.e, F.2.h, F.3.c, F.5.b, G.1.a, G.1.b, G.2.a, H.1.a, H.1.b, H.1.c, H.1.d.

Grow Your Own Valentine (holidays)

Materials: cellulose sponges (pink or red if possible), scissors, small red construction paper hearts, glue, toothpicks, marker, tray or dish to put the sponges in, grass seed-any quick germinating kind, mister or spray bottle, white paper bowls or jar lids.

Be sure to start this project 7-10 days before you want to send them home.
Cut sponges into heart shapes about 3-4 inches wide. Write each child's name on a small construction paper heart or have them write their own names on the hearts. Glue the hearts to a toothpick and stick it in a sponge. Have the children wet the sponges and place them on a tray or saucer. Sprinkle the grass seed over the tops of the sponges, covering the surface. Keep the heart gardens in a sunny window and water each day using a mister or spray bottle. The grass should sprout quickly and grow tall and green. Wait until it gets at least an inch or more tall before sending them home. Add more little hearts—one or two per garden. Glue the hearts to the top of the toothpicks and stick the other end into the sponge. Send the heart gardens home on Valentine's Day. Use heavy weight white paper bowls or clean jar lids to support the garden on its way home.

Topical signs to be learned: heart, Valentine, grass, grow, water, sun, name, give.
Indicators: A.1.a, A.1.b, A.1.c, A.1.d, A.2.a, A.2.b, A.2.c, B.1.c, B.2.a, B.2.b, B.2.c, C.2.b, D.1.b, D.2.c, D.2.d, F.1.b, F.2.b, F.2.d, F.2.e, F.2.h, F.3.a, F.3.c, F.4.b, G.1.a, G.1.b, G.2.a, G.3.a, H.1.b, H.1.d, H.2.a.

Haunted House (Halloween)

Materials: butcher paper, scissors, tape, black marker, crayons, white paper or construction paper, string or yarn, glue, Halloween cards (optional).

Cut two large sheets of butcher paper four feet long. Tape them on a wall, one above the

other. Draw a large haunted house on the paper. The children can color the haunted house. Cut windows on the haunted house. Cut only three sides of the windows so they can open and close. Make one window for each child (you can make multiple houses for larger groups). Place the paper, scissors and crayons on the table. Have the children draw creatures to live in the haunted house such as monsters, bats, spiders, witches, ghosts, vampires. The children cut out the creatures and choose a window in the haunted house. Tape a creature behind each window. The teacher can hide Halloween cards behind some additional windows, if desired. Sit in front of the haunted house. One child chooses a window and opens it. Play a memory game. See who can remember what creature is hiding behind what window. Leave the haunted house up till Halloween. Add something to the house each day such as spider webs, Halloween stickers, and any extra creepy crawlies drawn by the children.

Topical signs to be learned: Halloween, house, draw, crayon, spider, witch, window, door, hide, find, choose.
Indicators: A.1.b, A.1.c, A.1.d, A.2.a, A.2.b, A.2.c, B.1.c, C.2.b, F.1.b, F.2.b, F.2.c, F.2.d, F.2.e, F.2.h, F.3.c, G.1.a, G.1.b, G.2.a, H.1.a, H.1.b, H.1.c, H.1.d.

Helping Hand Father's Day Cards (holidays)
Materials: paper, stapler, construction paper, crayons or markers.

Talk about things the children can do around the house to help their dads (or mom's or grandparents, etc.). Have each child make handprints on three or four sheets of paper. Staple the papers together with a cover that says "Happy Father's Day." Children decorate their covers and sign their names. Recipients of the cards can tear out pages and give them to the children when they need helping hands.

Topical signs to be learned: father, day, help, hands, name.
Indicators: A.1.b, A.1.c, A.1.d, A.2.a, A.2.b, A.2.c, B.1.c, C.2.b, F.1.b, F.2.b, F.2.c, F.2.d, F.2.e, F.2.h, F.3.c, F.5.a, G.1.a, G.1.b, G.2.a, H.1.a, H.1.b, H.1.c, H.1.d.

Holiday Stocking (holidays)
Materials: Copy paper, construction paper, scissors (if old enough), glue sticks, paper cut outs and crayons.

Have the children color and decorate a stocking. The decorations are cut outs of holiday shapes such as a ball, reindeer, menorah, candle, etc. (older children may make the cut outs themselves).

Topical signs to be learned: stocking (sock), box, white, red.
Indicators: A.1.b, A.1.c, A.1.d, A.2.a, A.2.b, A.2.c, B.1.c, C.2.b, F.1.b, F.2.b, F.2.c, F.2.d, F.2.e, F.2.h, F.3.c, G.1.a, G.1.b, G.2.a, H.1.a, H.1.b, H.1.c, H.1.d.

Hot Air Balloons (transportation)
Materials: Balloon, paper mache' paint, glue, string, cup or berry basket, and smocks.

Paper mache' a blown up balloon. When dry, paint it, glue 3 pieces of string at the bottom & connect a paper cup with holes punched in the top (or use a berry basket) & tie.

Family, Home, Holidays, & Transportation

Topical signs to be learned: balloon, hot, paint, glue, string, basket, cup, dry.
Indicators: A.1.b, A.1.c, A.1.d, A.2.a, A.2.b, A.2.c, B.1.c, C.2.b, F.1.b, F.2.b, F.2.c, F.2.d, F.2.e, F.2.h, F.3.c, G.1.a, G.1.b, G.2.a, H.1.a, H.1.b, H.1.c, H.1.d.

Hot Air Balloon II (transportation)

Materials: white poster board, crayons or markers, paper lunch bag, and yarn.

Cut a large balloon shape from a white poster board & have kids decorate both sides with crayons or markers. Cut a paper lunch bag about 1/3 from the bottom for the basket. Punch 2 holes on the bottom of the balloon shape & on the short side of the lunch sack. Attach basket with yarn.

Topical signs to be learned: balloon, crayon, glue, string, basket.
Indicators: A.1.b, A.1.c, A.1.d, A.2.a, A.2.b, A.2.c, B.1.c, C.2.b, F.1.b, F.2.b, F.2.c, F.2.d, F.2.e, F.2.h, F.3.c, G.1.a, G.1.b, G.2.a, H.1.a, H.1.b, H.1.c, H.1.d.

Indian Corn (Thanksgiving)

Materials: pre-cut ear of corn shape, tissue paper (brown, orange, yellow, red), glue.

Have children tear tissue paper, crumple into balls and glue to pre-cut "ear."

Topical signs to be learned: corn, glue, brown, orange, yellow, red, Indian.
Indicators: A.1.b, A.1.c, A.1.d, A.2.a, A.2.b, A.2.c, B.1.c, C.2.b, F.1.b, F.2.b, F.2.c, F.2.d, F.2.e, F.2.h, F.3.c, G.1.a, G.1.b, G.2.a, H.1.a, H.1.b, H.1.c, H.1.d.

Indian Pudding (foods, Thanksgiving)

Materials: 3 ¾ cups milk, 1 cup cornmeal, 1 cup honey, ½ teaspoon salt, 4 eggs, 2 tablespoons butter, ½ teaspoon nutmeg, 1 cup raisins, ½ teaspoon soda, sauce pan, mixing spoon, whipped cream, baking pan, cooking spray/oil/shortening to grease pan.

Scald the milk, add cornmeal and stir constantly for five minutes. Let mixture cool until lukewarm. Add raisins, honey, beaten eggs, salt, and nutmeg. Bake in a greased pan for 1 ½ hours at 350 degrees. If batter stiffens too much during baking, add more milk. Allow pudding to cool a bit and serve it warm (or cold) with a dollop of whipped cream.
Topical signs to be learned: Indian, milk, corn, salt, eggs, butter, raisins, spoon, bake, hours.
Indicators: A.1.b, A.1.c, A.1.d, A.2.a, A.2.b, A.2.c, B.1.c, C.2.b, F.1.b, F.2.b, F.2.c, F.2.d, F.2.e, F.2.h, F.3.c, G.1.a, G.1.b, G.2.a, H.1.a, H.1.b, H.1.c, H.1.d.

Latkes/Potato Pancakes (Hanukkah)

Materials: grater, measuring spoons, mixing bowl, mixing spoon, 1 grated onion, 1 tsp. salt, 1 egg, 6 medium potatoes (washed, pared and grated), 3 T. flour, ½ tsp. baking powder, cooking oil, electric frying pan, paper towels, applesauce, sour cream, spoons and bowls.

Mix the onion, salt, and egg with the potatoes. Add flour and baking powder. Drop by spoonfuls into the hot oiled frying pan (be sure children are not close). Brown on both sides. Drain on paper towels. Serve with applesauce or sour cream.

Copyright © 2008 Time to Sign, Inc.

Topical signs to be learned: potato, cook (also: pancake), bowl, spoon, measure, egg, Hanukkah, eat, hot.
Indicators: A.1.b, A.1.c, A.1.d, A.2.a, A.2.b, A.2.c, B.1.c, C.2.b, F.1.b, F.2.b, F.2.c, F.2.d, F.2.e, F.2.h, F.3.c, G.1.a, G.1.b, G.2.a, H.1.a, H.1.b, H.1.c, H.1.d.

Liberty Bell (holidays)
Materials: tag board, brown paint, and smocks.

On tag board have children finger paint with brown paint. When dry, cut into the shape of a bell. Draw the crack.
Indicators: A.1.b, A.1.c, A.1.d, A.2.a, A.2.b, A.2.c, B.1.c, C.2.b, F.1.b, F.2.b, F.2.c, F.2.d, F.2.e, F.2.h, F.3.c, G.1.a, G.1.b, G.2.a, H.1.a, H.1.b, H.1.c, H.1.d.

Little Pebble Family Home (home, family)
Materials: oval pebbles or smooth stones, newspaper, acrylic paint, paintbrushes, scissors, tape, glue, shoebox or any strong box, knife to cut the box (adult use only), decorating materials for people or houses (aluminum foil, cardboard, carpet scraps, cotton balls, craft eyes, flooring scraps, glitter glue, markers, paper scraps, permanent markers, plastic wrap, sewing trim, sticky dots, wallpaper scraps, yarn).

Paint the rocks like a family on a newspaper covered surface. Have the bigger rocks be the parents, the smaller ones children and the tiniest one the baby. Let dry. When dry the pebble family can be played with as is or decorated further. Glue on decorative features such as yarn hair, cotton beard, googly eyes, sticky dot cheeks, and glitter clothes. Let dry again.

Build a house for the pebble family from a shoe box or sturdy box. Cut out windows and doors where the child designates (adult only). Decorate as desired (Examples: plastic wrap taped to windows. Fabric scraps glued to windows for curtains. Wallpaper covering the walls. Carpet scraps for flooring. Furniture built from cardboard, glue and tape.)
Have the pebble family move into their new home and start having adventures.

Topical signs to be learned: family signs, home signs, box, paint, paper, glue, scissors.
Indicators: A.1.b, A.1.c, A.1.d, A.2.a, A.2.b, A.2.c, B.1.c, C.2.b, F.1.b, F.2.b, F.2.c, F.2.d, F.2.e, F.2.h, F.3.c, F.5.a, G.1.a, G.1.b, G.2.a, H.1.a, H.1.b, H.1.c, H.1.d.

Miniature Christmas Trees (holidays)
Materials: large pine cone, aluminum foil, jar lid slightly larger than the base of the pine cone, glue, paint, tinsel, sequins, glitter.

Cover the lid of a jar with aluminum foil. Glue the base of the pine cone to the top of the foil-covered lid. Use paint, glitter, sequins, or tinsel to decorate the tree.

Topical signs to be learned: Christmas, tree, decorate, glue.
Indicators: A.1.b, A.1.c, A.1.d, A.2.a, A.2.b, A.2.c, B.1.c, C.2.b, F.1.b, F.2.b, F.2.c, F.2.d, F.2.e, F.2.h, F.3.c, G.1.a, G.1.b, G.2.a, H.1.a, H.1.b, H.1.c, H.1.d.

New Year's Collage (holiday, New Year's)
Materials: colored construction paper, hole punch, glue, dark blue or black construction paper, silver tinsel, brush for glue.

Family, Home, Holidays, & Transportation

Make "confetti" by using a hole punch on brightly colored construction paper. Brush glue over the dark sheets of construction paper. Drop strands of tinsel on top of the glue and sprinkle small handfuls of confetti.

Topical signs to be learned: New Year's, glue, paper, color signs.
Indicators: A.1.b, A.1.c, A.1.d, A.2.a, A.2.b, A.2.c, B.1.c, C.2.b, F.1.b, F.2.b, F.2.c, F.2.d, F.2.e, F.2.h, F.3.c, G.1.a, G.1.b, G.2.a, H.1.a, H.1.b, H.1.c, H.1.d.

New Year's Paper Lanterns (holidays)
Materials: paper, scissors, glue; crayons, markers, or colored pencils (optional).

Fold an oblong sheet of paper in half, then make equal cuts from the folded edge, taking care not to snip right across the paper. Open it out and glue the edges together, then cut a small strip of paper for the handle and glue it to each side at the top. If you want to color it, it's best to do so before you open it out.
Use the paper lanterns to decorate the classroom by hanging them from the ceiling or making a string of paper lanterns and hanging them around.

Topical signs to be learned: paper, scissors, crayon, New Year's.
Indicators: A.1.b, A.1.c, A.1.d, A.2.a, A.2.b, A.2.c, B.1.c, C.2.b, F.1.b, F.2.b, F.2.c, F.2.d, F.2.e, F.2.h, F.3.c, G.1.a, G.1.b, G.2.a, H.1.a, H.1.b, H.1.c, H.1.d.

No-Sew Stockings (holidays)
Materials: felt, scissors, fake fur scraps, glue, pinking shears, rubber cement or hot glue gun, glitter or glitter pens (optional), ribbon or yarn (optional).

Using scrap felt pieces, cut out and glue together the pieces to make little felt Christmas pictures (such as a little Santa Claus face, a wreath, a candle, a star, a toy, a Christmas tree, a bell etc.) Using pinking shears to cut from red, green, or white felt two large identical stocking shapes for each stocking. Apply a 1-inch wide strip of rubber cement along the inside of each stocking—NOT including the top edges. Let the cement dry and then, making certain that edges match, press stockings together firmly! Place the stockings flat under heavy weights (books) for one night. OR use a hot glue gun to glue the pieces together (Have an adult do this to prevent children from burning their fingers or hands). Glue a small loop of ribbon or yarn to one corner of the stocking if you wish to hang the stocking. Use white glue to adhere the felt decorations. Add (2-3") fake fur trim to the top of the stocking. Children can print their name or add other decorations to their stockings in white glue sprinkled with glitter or glitter pens.

You can give small presents or candy to the children to put in their stockings. Or the children can make the stockings as gifts for others.

Topical signs to be learned: Christmas, stocking (sock), scissors, glue, decorate, candle, star, tree, bell, red, green, white, name.
Indicators: A.1.b, A.1.c, A.1.d, A.2.a, A.2.b, A.2.c, B.1.c, C.2.b, F.1.b, F.2.b, F.2.c, F.2.d, F.2.e, F.2.h, F.3.c, G.1.a, G.1.b, G.2.a, H.1.a, H.1.b, H.1.c, H.1.d.

Family, Home, Holidays, & Transportation

Paper Plate Wreath (holidays)
Materials: Paper, scissors (if old enough), glue sticks, paper cut outs and crayons.
Have the children decorate a paper plate with the center cut out (older children may cut out the center). Have ornaments, pine cones, bows and pictures they can color and attach. OR trace children's hands and cut out in various shades of green and glue together or glue to paper plate.

Topical signs to be learned: paper, plate, circle, scissors, glue, crayons, ribbon.
Indicators: A.1.b, A.1.c, A.1.d, A.2.a, A.2.b, A.2.c, B.1.c, C.2.b, F.1.b, F.2.b, F.2.c, F.2.d, F.2.e, F.2.h, F.3.c, G.1.a, G.1.b, G.2.a, H.1.a, H.1.b, H.1.c, H.1.d.

Paper Rockets (transportation)
Materials: different colored construction paper, scissors, white paper, tape, star stickers.

Cut a 2" x 4" colored construction paper rectangle for each child. Cut a large moon shape from the white paper. Tape it on a wall.
Place colored construction paper and pieces of tape on the table. Each child chooses a piece of paper and puts star stickers on it. Roll the sheet of paper to make a tube and tape the ends together. This is the rocket ship body. Place the rectangular pieces of paper on the table. Each child chooses one and forms a cone shape. Tape the ends together. Tape the cone over one end of the rocket ship body.

Topical signs to be learned: paper, scissors, rectangle, rocket, earth, moon, star, astronaut.
Indicators: A.1.b, A.1.c, A.1.d, A.2.a, A.2.b, A.2.c, B.1.c, C.2.b, F.1.b, F.2.b, F.2.c, F.2.d, F.2.e, F.2.h, F.3.c, G.1.a, G.1.b, G.2.a, H.1.a, H.1.b, H.1.c, H.1.d.

Passport, Please (transportation, travel)
Materials: paper, markers or crayons, glue or stapler, instant camera, scissors, rubber stamps and stamp pad (optional), clear contact paper (optional)
Cut two pieces of paper 4 x 8". Glue or staple the two pieces together and fold in half to make a booklet. On the front with markers or crayons have each child write their name and "PASSPORT" on the front and below that a made up passport number. On the firsts inside page on separate lines write first name, last name, town, and country. On the opposite page glue a photo or draw a self-portrait and draw a box around it. Cover the photos or pictures with clear contact paper for protection, if desired. Children can use rubber stamps to stamp their passports before entering or when leaving the plane.

Topical signs to be learned: paper, scissors, write, name, first, last, country, number, picture, glue, draw.
Indicators: A.1.b, A.1.c, A.1.d, A.2.a, A.2.b, A.2.c, B.1.c, C.2.b, F.1.b, F.2.b, F.2.c, F.2.d, F.2.e, F.2.h, F.3.c, G.1.a, G.1.b, G.2.a, H.1.a, H.1.b, H.1.c, H.1.d.

Pet Baskets (home, pets)
Materials: cardboard box, poster board, construction paper scraps, markers, animal stickers, cotton balls or fiber batting, pieces of fabric, glue, scissors.

Cut out an animal shape for each child from poster board or have a class stuffed animal or animal from home for each child. Have each child decorate a box and line it with soft

Copyright © 2008 Time to Sign, Inc.

Family, Home, Holidays, & Transportation

material as a sleeping basket for their "pet". Encourage them to pick materials and colors they think their pet will like.
Topical signs to be learned: pet signs, bed, sleep, paper, glue, scissors, color signs, like.
Indicators: A.1.b, A.1.c, A.1.d, A.2.a, A.2.b, A.2.c, B.1.c, C.2.b, F.1.b, F.2.b, F.2.c, F.2.d, F.2.e, F.2.h, F.3.c, G.1.a, G.1.b, G.2.a, H.1.a, H.1.b, H.1.c, H.1.d.

Picture Frame (family)

Materials: craft sticks, paint, paintbrushes, smocks, old puzzle pieces, construction paper or poster board rectangles, and pictures of children or take instant or digital pictures so it's a surprise for mom.

Make a picture frame by using popsicle sticks and old puzzle pieces. Glue sticks together to form a frame. Then glue old puzzle pieces onto the sticks. Place a picture of child inside and glue a piece of construction paper or poster board to back of sticks.

Topical signs to be learned: paint, puzzle, glue, picture, paper.
Indicators: A.1.b, A.1.c, A.1.d, A.2.a, A.2.b, A.2.c, B.1.c, C.2.b, F.1.b, F.2.b, F.2.c, F.2.d, F.2.e, F.2.h, F.3.c, F.5.a, G.1.a, G.1.b, G.2.a, H.1.a, H.1.b, H.1.c, H.1.d.

Printed Wrapping Paper (holidays)

Materials: red or green tissue paper, thick poster paint (white, green, or red), glitter (optional), holiday stamps or styrofoam meet tray, glue, straight pin, and cork.

If making your own stamps, cut out small star, bbell, tree or other holiday shapes from the styrofoam meat trays. Use white glue and a straight pin to fasten each stamp to a cork. Let dry.

Dip the stamps in poster paint and stamp at random over the surface of the tissue paper. A light sprinkling of glitter finishes the wrapping paper, if desired.

Topical signs to be learned: paper, paint, glue, Christmas, shape signs, red, green, white.
Indicators: A.1.b, A.1.c, A.1.d, A.2.a, A.2.b, A.2.c, B.1.c, C.2.b, F.1.b, F.2.b, F.2.c, F.2.d, F.2.e, F.2.h, F.3.c, G.1.a, G.1.b, G.2.a, H.1.a, H.1.b, H.1.c, H.1.d.

Pumpkin Painting (Halloween)

Materials: pumpkins, orange and black paint, paintbrushes, and smocks.

Start with white construction paper. Have children paint pumpkins orange, when dry they can add facial features with black paint. For younger children you can start with orange paper and simply pant in the black facial features.

Topical signs to be learned: pumpkin, orange, black, white, paper, paint, face.
Indicators: A.1.b, A.1.c, A.1.d, A.2.a, A.2.b, A.2.c, B.1.c, C.2.b, F.1.b, F.2.b, F.2.c, F.2.d, F.2.e, F.2.h, F.3.c, G.1.a, G.1.b, G.2.a, H.1.a, H.1.b, H.1.c, H.1.d.

Rocket Ship -Box (transportation)

Materials: 3-4 large cardboard boxes, duct tape, paint, paintbrushes, colored construction paper, star stickers, tape, poster board or butcher paper, scissors or box cutter (adult use only).

Copyright © 2008 Time to Sign, Inc.

Family, Home, Holidays, & Transportation

Tape the boxes on top of each other with duct tape. If the boxes are large enough, cut an opening on the bottom box large enough for a child. Paint the boxes. Cut out shapes from colored construction paper and tape them on or inside the boxes for control buttons. Place starts on the box. Make a giant cone shape from the poster board or butcher paper and tape it to the top of the boxes.

Topical signs to be learned: rocket, box, paint, paper, star.
Indicators: A.1.b, A.1.c, A.1.d, A.2.a, A.2.b, A.2.c, B.1.c, C.2.b, F.1.b, F.2.b, F.2.c, F.2.d, F.2.e, F.2.h, F.3.c, G.1.a, G.1.b, G.2.a, H.1.a, H.1.b, H.1.c, H.1.d.

Sailboat (ocean, transportation)
Materials: Margarine tub, clay, paper, crayons and markers, and straw.

Press a ball of clay in the bottom of a margarine tub. Insert a straw in the clay; then tape a decorated paper into the top of the straw.

Topical signs to be learned: sailboat, paper.
Indicators: A.1.b, A.1.c, A.1.d, A.2.a, A.2.b, A.2.c, B.1.c, C.2.b, F.1.b, F.2.b, F.2.c, F.2.d, F.2.e, F.2.h, F.3.c, G.1.a, G.1.b, G.2.a, H.1.a, H.1.b, H.1.c, H.1.d.

Sailing Along (transportation)
Materials: white construction paper, marker, scissors, empty milk cartons, straws, tape, crayons, water table or large pan of water, masking tape.

Draw a large triangle on a sheet of white construction paper and cut it out to make a sail. Make one for each child (or trace triangles onto construction paper and give to children to cut out). Cut milk cartons 3" from the bottom. Tape a straw against the inside of the carton to make a mast for the sailboat. Have children decorate their sails with crayons. When finished with the sails, tape them to the mast.
Children can take turns placing their boat in the water table or large pan of water and making them sail. Children can name their boats and place the name on a piece of masking tape on the side of their boat.
You can also have children draw people on construction paper and cut them out to go sailing in their boats.

Topical signs to be learned: boat, sailboat, water, ocean, water table, name, paper, scissors, crayon.

Indicators: A.1.b, A.1.c, A.1.d, A.2.a, A.2.b, A.2.c, B.1.c, C.2.b, F.1.b, F.2.b, F.2.c, F.2.d, F.2.e, F.2.h, F.3.c, G.1.a, G.1.b, G.2.a, H.1.a, H.1.b, H.1.c, H.1.d.

Santa Puppet (holidays)
Materials: Copy paper, construction paper, paper bag, scissors (if old enough), glue sticks, paper cut outs and crayons.

Have the children color a 2-part Santa cut out and glue it to a paper bag.
Or
Have the children put together various different shapes and color them. The hat, face, and beard for the top of the bag. The coat, belt, pants, and shoes for the bottom of the bag.

Copyright © 2008 Time to Sign, Inc.

Family, Home, Holidays, & Transportation

Topical signs to be learned: bag, paper, red, white, black, glue, scissors, crayon, paper.
Indicators: A.1.b, A.1.c, A.1.d, A.2.a, A.2.b, A.2.c, B.1.c, C.2.b, F.1.b, F.2.b, F.2.c, F.2.d, F.2.e, F.2.h, F.3.c, G.1.a, G.1.b, G.2.a, H.1.a, H.1.b, H.1.c, H.1.d.

Shamrocks (St. Patrick's Day)
Materials: pre-drawn shamrock shapes, pistachio pudding and smocks.

Use pistachio pudding to paint shamrocks, can be on copy paper with shamrock shape or on pre-cut shamrock shape.

Topical signs to be learned: green, paper, St. Patrick's Day.

Indicators: A.1.b, A.1.c, A.1.d, A.2.a, A.2.b, A.2.c, B.1.c, C.2.b, F.1.b, F.2.b, F.2.c, F.2.d, F.2.e, F.2.h, F.3.c, G.1.a, G.1.b, G.2.a, H.1.a, H.1.b, H.1.c, H.1.d.

Shoe Box Train (transportation)
Materials: show boxes, tempera paints, paintbrushes, construction paper, scissors, glue.

Have children paint their shoe box(s). When the paint is dry, cut out construction paper wheels and windows and glue them to the show box train.

Topical signs to be learned: train, box, paint, paper, scissors, glue, window, wheel, circle, square/rectangle.

Indicators: A.1.b, A.1.c, A.1.d, A.2.a, A.2.b, A.2.c, B.1.c, C.2.b, F.1.b, F.2.b, F.2.c, F.2.d, F.2.e, F.2.h, F.3.c, G.1.a, G.1.b, G.2.a, H.1.a, H.1.b, H.1.c, H.1.d.

Snack Food Containers (holidays)
Materials: coffee cans or other containers with plastic lids, construction paper, crayons, markers or paint; scissors, tape or glue, snack foods (granola, popcorn, snack mixes, cookies, etc.)

Cut construction paper to fit around the sides of the containers. Have the children decorate their papers with crayons, markers, or paints. Then tape or glue the papers around the sides of the containers. If desired, let children will their containers with a snack (can be something purchased or homemade). Snack food containers make great gifts for father's day, Christmas, or other special occasions.

Topical signs to be learned: paper, scissors, crayon, paint, glue, snack, give.
Indicators: A.1.b, A.1.c, A.1.d, A.2.a, A.2.b, A.2.c, B.1.c, C.2.b, F.1.b, F.2.b, F.2.c, F.2.d, F.2.e, F.2.h, F.3.c, G.1.a, G.1.b, G.2.a, H.1.a, H.1.b, H.1.c, H.1.d.

Sponge Trees (Christmas)
Materials: sponges cut into Christmas tree shapes, drawing paper, green tempera paint.

Place paint, sponges, and paper out for the children to use. Have the children dip the sponges in the green paint and create designs on their paper. Older children can add details to the picture when dry.

Copyright © 2008 Time to Sign, Inc.

Family, Home, Holidays, & Transportation

Topical signs to be learned: Christmas, tree, paint, paper, dry, green.
Indicators: A.1.b, A.1.c, A.1.d, A.2.a, A.2.b, A.2.c, B.1.c, C.2.b, F.1.b, F.2.b, F.2.c, F.2.d, F.2.e, F.2.h, F.3.c, G.1.a, G.1.b, G.2.a, H.1.a, H.1.b, H.1.c, H.1.d.

Spool Painting (transportation)

Materials: construction paper, scissors, tempera paint, styrofoam trays or paint trays, spools.

Cut construction paper into simple bus shapes or other vehicle shape. Have children use the spools to make wheel shapes with the paint all over their vehicles.

Topical signs to be learned: wheel, bus (or other vehicle), circle, paint.
Indicators: A.1.b, A.1.c, A.1.d, A.2.a, A.2.b, A.2.c, B.1.c, C.2.b, F.1.b, F.2.b, F.2.c, F.2.d, F.2.e, F.2.h, F.3.c, G.1.a, G.1.b, G.2.a, H.1.a, H.1.b, H.1.c, H.1.d.

Stars and Stripes Collages (holidays)

Materials: 9"x12" blue construction paper, red and white construction paper, glue, silver star stickers.

Cut 1"x9" strips from the white and red construction paper (or draw lines and let children cut them out). Set out glue and silver star stickers and let children glue paper strips and place stickers on the blue construction paper any way they wish to create their own stars and stripes design.

Topical signs to be learned: Independence day, flag, star, red, blue, white, silver, glue, paper, scissors.
Indicators: A.1.b, A.1.c, A.1.d, A.2.a, A.2.b, A.2.c, B.1.c, C.2.b, F.1.b, F.2.b, F.2.c, F.2.d, F.2.e, F.2.h, F.3.c, G.1.a, G.1.b, G.2.a, H.1.a, H.1.b, H.1.c, H.1.d.

Star of David I (holidays)

Materials: construction paper and scissors or popsicle sticks, paint and brushes, glitter glue, glue or glue sticks, Q-tips.
Cut out two triangles and glue them together to form a star of David. Or glue popsicle sticks together into two triangles and glue those triangles together into a star of David. Decorate it by using glitter glue, glitter and glue, or paint using Q-tips or paint brushes to paint.

Topical signs to be learned: paper, scissors, glue, triangle, star, paint, decorate.
Indicators: A.1.b, A.1.c, A.1.d, A.2.a, A.2.b, A.2.c, B.1.c, C.2.b, F.1.b, F.2.b, F.2.c, F.2.d, F.2.e, F.2.h, F.3.c, G.1.a, G.1.b, G.2.a, H.1.a, H.1.b, H.1.c, H.1.d.

Star of David II (Hanukkah)

Materials: construction paper triangles (two for each child), glue, paper.

Demonstrate how to place two triangles together to form a Star of David. The children create their star and glue it onto another piece of paper.

Topical signs to be learned: Hanukkah, star, glue, paper, triangle.
Indicators: A.1.b, A.1.c, A.1.d, A.2.a, A.2.b, A.2.c, B.1.c, C.2.b, F.1.b, F.2.b, F.2.c, F.2.d, F.2.e, F.2.h, F.3.c, G.1.a, G.1.b, G.2.a, H.1.a, H.1.b, H.1.c, H.1.d.

Family, Home, Holidays, & Transportation

Stars (holidays)
Materials: black construction paper, sponges in the shape of stars, and smocks.

Sponge paint a night sky.

Topical signs to be learned: black, sky, star, night, paint.
Indicators: A.1.b, A.1.c, A.1.d, A.2.a, A.2.b, A.2.c, B.1.c, C.2.b, F.1.b, F.2.b, F.2.c, F.2.d, F.2.e, F.2.h, F.3.c, G.1.a, G.1.b, G.2.a, H.1.a, H.1.b, H.1.c, H.1.d.

String of Hearts (holidays)
Materials: colored construction paper, black felt pen, scissors, yarn, hole punchers, tape.

Cut 4" x 4" squares of construction paper, at least 10 for each child. Draw a heart shape on each square. Cut a 3' piece of yarn for each child. Place the paper hearts and scissors on the work surface. Have children cut out the hearts and make their hearts into a pile. Using a hole punch, making a hole at the top of the hearts. String the hearts on the yearn. When a string of hearts is finished, the teacher can tie or tape each heart in place on the string, about an inch or two apart. Have child print their name or you print their name on one of the hearts. The strings of hearts can be used to decorate the classroom. You can have children count how many hearts are on each string of hearts.

Topical signs to be learned: heart, scissors, paper, string, number signs.
Indicators: A.1.b, A.1.c, A.1.d, A.2.a, A.2.b, A.2.c, B.1.c, C.1.a, C.1.b, C.1.d, C.2.b, F.1.b, F.2.b, F.2.c, F.2.d, F.2.e, F.2.h, F.3.c, G.1.a, G.1.b, G.2.a, H.1.a, H.1.b, H.1.c, H.1.d.

Thanksgiving Dinner (holidays, food)
Materials: magazines, small paper cups, glue, scissors, paper plates, cotton swabs.

Tear out magazine pages with food pictures on them. Pour glue into paper cups, one per child. Have children cut out the food pictures and glue them onto a paper plate using the cotton swabs to spread the glue.
Topical signs to be learned: food signs, Thanksgiving, dinner, plate, glue, scissors.
Indicators: A.1.b, A.1.c, A.1.d, A.2.a, A.2.b, A.2.c, B.1.c, C.1.a, C.1.b, C.1.d, C.2.b, F.1.b, F.2.b, F.2.c, F.2.d, F.2.e, F.2.h, F.3.c, G.1.a, G.1.b, G.2.a, H.1.a, H.1.b, H.1.c, H.1.d.

Train Cars (Transportation)
Materials: construction paper rectangle for each child, crayons, 2 wheels per child, glue.

Decorate rectangles with crayons. Glue on wheels.

Topical signs to be learned: rectangle, wheels, car, crayon, glue.
Indicators: A.1.b, A.1.c, A.1.d, A.2.a, A.2.b, A.2.c, B.1.c, C.1.a, C.1.b, C.1.d, C.2.b, F.1.b, F.2.b, F.2.c, F.2.d, F.2.e, F.2.h, F.3.c, G.1.a, G.1.b, G.2.a, H.1.a, H.1.b, H.1.c, H.1.d.

Transportation Mural (transportation)
Materials: large rolled bulletin board paper, crayons and markers, old magazines, and glue.

Using the rolled paper have students plan and draw a scene. Share the jobs - one can draw

a train track while another draws a road, another clouds, maybe a lake, house or trees. On days to come have them gradually fill up the mural with cut and paste vehicles, airplanes, trains, cars, boats, trucks or even hot air balloons from old magazines!

Topical signs to be learned: paper, plan, draw, share, transportation signs, scissors.
Indicators: A.1.b, A.1.c, A.1.d, A.2.a, A.2.b, A.2.c, B.1.c, C.1.a, C.1.b, C.1.d, C.2.b, F.1.b, F.2.b, F.2.c, F.2.d, F.2.e, F.2.h, F.3.c, G.1.a, G.1.b, G.2.a, H.1.a, H.1.b, H.1.c, H.1.d.

Tree Ornaments (holidays)
Materials: Paper, scissors (if old enough), glue sticks, paper cut outs and crayons.

Have the children decorate round cut shapes using crayons, glitter, and little foil holiday shapes (older children can cut out their own shapes or decorate white Styrofoam balls). Attach strings to the top.

Topical signs to be learned: ball, , string, tree, glue, crayon, and paper.
Indicators: A.1.b, A.1.c, A.1.d, A.2.a, A.2.b, A.2.c, B.1.c, C.1.a, C.1.b, C.1.d, C.2.b, F.1.b, F.2.b, F.2.c, F.2.d, F.2.e, F.2.h, F.3.c, G.1.a, G.1.b, G.2.a, H.1.a, H.1.b, H.1.c, H.1.d.

Turkey Handprint (Thanksgiving)
Materials: brown paint, feathers (use feathers that you can buy at a local craft store or you can also buy a feather duster from the $1 store and have the children pull out the feathers from the duster), glue sticks, and smocks.

Trace or paint child's hand print. Use feathers that you can buy at a local craft store. (You can also buy a feather duster from the dollar store and have the children pull out the feathers, then glue onto handprint.)

Topical signs to be learned: hand, paint, feather, turkey.
Indicators: A.1.b, A.1.c, A.1.d, A.2.a, A.2.b, A.2.c, B.1.c, C.1.a, C.1.b, C.1.d, C.2.b, F.1.b, F.2.b, F.2.c, F.2.d, F.2.e, F.2.h, F.3.c, G.1.a, G.1.b, G.2.a, H.1.a, H.1.b, H.1.c, H.1.d.

Valentine's Card (Valentine's Day)
Materials: pre-cut hearts, red paint and smocks.

Have children make thumbprints on heart shapes and label with "Thumbbody Loves You".

Topical signs to be learned: heart, love, you, red, paint.
Indicators: A.1.b, A.1.c, A.1.d, A.2.a, A.2.b, A.2.c, B.1.c, C.1.a, C.1.b, C.1.d, C.2.b, F.1.b, F.2.a, F.2.b, F.2.c, F.2.d, F.2.e, F.2.h, F.3.c, F.5.a G.1.a, G.1.b, G.2.a, H.1.a, H.1.b, H.1.c, H.1.d.

Valentine Hearts (holidays)
Materials: red, white and pink construction paper; scissors, white glue or glue sticks, paper doilies, red felt pen, scraps of wrapping paper, foil papers, etc.

Show the children how to cut hearts on a fold. Fold the paper, and along the fold draw an "elephant's ear." Cut this out on the fold to create a symmetrical heart. Vary the size to make larger or smaller hearts. Glue different color and size hearts on top of each other, on

Family, Home, Holidays, & Transportation

dollies, etc. Let the children have fun. Write messages with a red felt pen or have children write the messages themselves.

Topical signs to be learned: Valentine, heart, red, white, pink, scissors, glue, write, love.
Indicators: A.1.b, A.1.c, A.1.d, A.2.a, A.2.b, A.2.c, B.1.c, C.1.a, C.1.b, C.1.d, C.2.b, F.1.b, F.2.b, F.2.c, F.2.d, F.2.e, F.2.h, F.3.c, G.1.a, G.1.b, G.2.a, H.1.a, H.1.b, H.1.c, H.1.d.

Wheel Mural (transportation)

Materials: paper towels, styrofoam trays or other dish for paint, toys with wheels, brown craft paper, pasta wheel shapes, glue.

Place a paper towel on one side of a tray as a blotter and paint on the other side. Have the children place a toy in the paint and then make wheel tracks on the paper. Compare the wheel tracks. Then given wheel pasta and have them glue them onto their paper to decorate their wheel murals.

Topical signs to be learned: wheel, paint, car, truck.
Indicators: A.1.b, A.1.c, A.1.d, A.2.a, A.2.b, A.2.c, B.1.c, C.1.a, C.1.b, C.1.d, C.2.b, F.1.b, F.2.b, F.2.c, F.2.d, F.2.e, F.2.h, F.3.c, G.1.a, G.1.b, G.2.a, H.1.a, H.1.b, H.1.c, H.1.d.

Home Signs - Señales Del Hogar

Family, Home, Holidays, & Transportation

51

Rub the "A" handshapes on the chest near the shoulder, palms facing in.

[Also: scrub, wash]

bathing - bañarse

Copyright © 2008 Time to Sign, Inc.

52   **Family, Home, Holidays, & Transportation**

Place the slightly curved dominant "5" handshape on the same-sided cheek and tilt the head to the side.

[As if laying down your head on the hand]

bed – cama

Copyright © 2008 Time to Sign, Inc.

Family, Home, Holidays, & Transportation

53

Tap the fingers of the "H" handshape on top of the reference "H" handshape, palms facing down, with a double movement.

[As if two legs are dangling from a bench]

chair - silla

Copyright © 2008 Time to Sign, Inc.

Family, Home, Holidays, & Transportation

Start with both hands facing up and touching in front of the chest,, palms facing forward, move the dominant hand out while turning sideways with a double movement.

door - puerta

Family, Home, Holidays, & Transportation

55

Place the tips of the flattened "O" handshape against the mouth and then the cheek, palm facing down (or place the flat hand on the cheek).

home – hogar

Copyright © 2008 Time to Sign, Inc.

Family, Home, Holidays, & Transportation

Start with the fingertips of both open hands touching in front of the upper body, palms facing one another, bring the hands at a downward angle outward to in front of each shoulder and then straight down.

[Indicates the shape of a house]

house – casa

Family, Home, Holidays, & Transportation

Move both "A" handshapes, palms facing in, upwards simultaneously from in front of either side of the waist.

live – vivir

Family, Home, Holidays, & Transportation

Place both hands, palm facing each other, the dominant hand above the reference hand, below the cheek on reference side of the body, move slightly together and apart a few times.

[As plumping a pillow a few times between them]

pillow – almohada

Family, Home, Holidays, & Transportation

Start with both open handshapes in front of each side of the body, palms facing each other and fingers pointing forward, move the hands in opposite directions by the bending the wrists, ending the with the reference hand near the chest and the dominant hand several inches forward of the reference hand, both palms facing in.

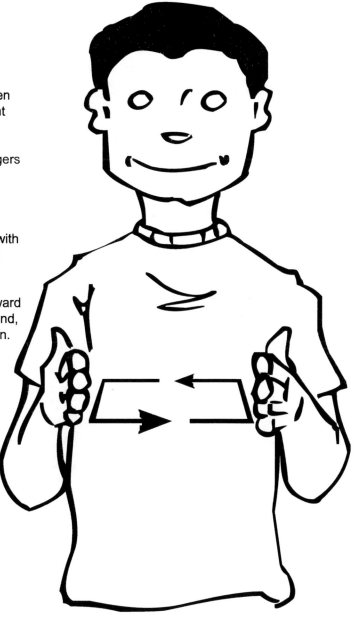

room – cuarto

Copyright © 2008 Time to Sign, Inc.

Family, Home, Holidays, & Transportation

Wipe the fingers of the bent dominant handshape on the palm of the open reference hand from the fingers to the heel of the hand with a double movement, bending the dominant hand fingers back into the palm during each of the double movements.

soap – jabón

Family, Home, Holidays, & Transportation

Begin with the dominant "5" handshape in front of the face, palm facing in, pull down into a flattened "O" handshape while bringing head down.

sleepy - sueño

Family, Home, Holidays, & Transportation

Pat the forearm of the bent dominant arm with a double movement on the bent reference arm held across the chest, palms facing down.

table - mesa

Family, Home, Holidays, & Transportation

63

Scratch the upper chest near the shoulders repeatedly with both "5" handshapes crossed in front of chest at the wrists, palms facing in.

[As if giving a bear hug]

teddy bear – oso de peluche

Copyright © 2008 Time to Sign, Inc.

Family, Home, Holidays, & Transportation

Place the thumb of the dominant "Y" handshape on the ear and the little finger at the mouth, palm facing in.

[As if talking on the phone]

[Also: call]

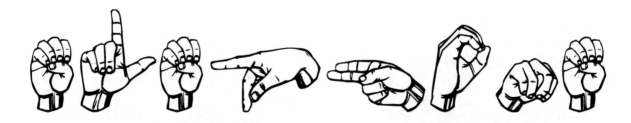

telephone – teléfono

Family, Home, Holidays, & Transportation

Move the dominant "T" handshape, palm facing forward, from side to side in front of the dominant shoulder with a repeated shaking movement.

[Also: bathroom]

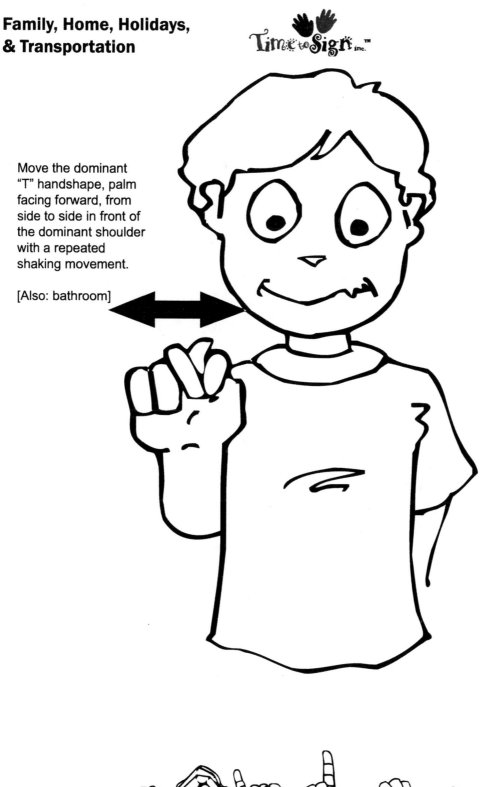

toilet - inodoro

Family, Home, Holidays, & Transportation

Swing both "T" handshapes up and down by twisting the wrists in front of each side of the body with a repeated movement.

toy – juguete

Family, Home, Holidays, & Transportation

Start with the dominant open hand just above the reference open hand, palms facing in and fingers pointing in opposite directions, bring the little finger side of the dominant open hand down sharply with a double movement on the index-finger side of the reference open hand.

[As if closing a window]

window - ventana

Family Signs - Señales De Familia

Family, Home, Holidays, & Transportation

69

Shake the dominant "A" handshape, palm facing forward, near the dominant cheek.

aunt – tía

Copyright © 2008 Time to Sign, Inc.

Family, Home, Holidays, & Transportation

With the bent dominant arm cradled on the bent reference arm, both palms facing up, swing the arms to the dominant and reference in front of the body with a double movement.

[As if cradling a baby in your arms]

baby - bebé

Family, Home, Holidays, & Transportation

71

Start with the index-finger side of the dominant flattened "C" handshape near the dominant side of the forehead, palm facing reference, close the fingers to the thumb with a repeated movement.

[As if grasping the bill of a baseball cap]

boy – niño

Copyright © 2008 Time to Sign, Inc.

Family, Home, Holidays, & Transportation

First move with the index-finger side of the dominant "C" handshape near the dominant side of the forehead, now close the fingers to the thumb with a repeated movement. Then place both index fingers side by side, pointing to the front, palms facing down.

[Sign: boy + same]

brother - hermano

Family, Home, Holidays, & Transportation

Move the dominant "C", palm facing reference side, with a shaking movement near the dominant side of the forehead for male cousin, and near the dominant chin for female cousin.

cousin - primo(a)

Copyright © 2008 Time to Sign, Inc.

74  **Family, Home, Holidays, & Transportation**

Begin with both "F" handshapes touching in front of the chest, palms facing each other, bring the hands away from each other in outward arcs while turning the palms in, ending with the little fingers touching.

family - familia

Copyright © 2008 Time to Sign, Inc.

Family, Home, Holidays, & Transportation

75

Tap the thumb of the dominant "5" handshape against the middle of the forehead, palm facing reference, with a double movement.

father - padre

Copyright © 2008 Time to Sign, Inc.

Family, Home, Holidays, & Transportation

Move the thumb of the dominant "A" handshape, downward on the dominant cheek to the dominant side of the chin.

girl - niña

Family, Home, Holidays, & Transportation

Place the thumb of the dominant "5" handshape, palm facing reference, on the forehead and then bounce forward from forehead twice.

[Origin: One generation away from father]

grandfather – abuelo

Family, Home, Holidays, & Transportation

Place the thumb of the "5" handshape, palm facing reference, on the chin and then bounce forward twice.

[Origin: One generation away from mother]

grandmother – abuela

Family, Home, Holidays, & Transportation

79

The hands hold the upper arms as if hugging one's self.

hug – abrazo

Copyright © 2008 Time to Sign, Inc.

Family, Home, Holidays, & Transportation

Hold up the dominant hand with the thumb, index finger, and little finger extended, palm facing forward, in front of the dominant shoulder.

I love you – te quiero

Family, Home, Holidays, & Transportation

Touch the fingertips of the dominant flattened "O" handshape, palm facing in, to the dominant side of the mouth, then open the dominant hand and place it against the dominant cheek.

kiss – beso

82   **Family, Home, Holidays, & Transportation**

Tap the thumb of the dominant "5" handshape, palm facing reference, against the chin.

mother - madre

Copyright © 2008 Time to Sign, Inc.

Family, Home, Holidays, & Transportation

First move the thumb of the dominant "A" hand, palm facing reference side, downward on the dominant cheek to the dominant side of the chin. Then place both index fingers side by side, pointing to the front, palms facing down.

[Sign: girl + same]

sister - hermana

84

Family, Home, Holidays, & Transportation

Shake the dominant "U" handshape, palm facing forward, by the side of the dominant forehead.

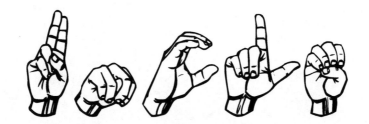

uncle - tío

Copyright © 2008 Time to Sign, Inc.

Family, Home, Holidays, & Transportation

Pet Signs

-

Señales De Animales

Family, Home, Holidays, & Transportation

Begin with the fingertips of both curved "5" handshapes on the chest near each shoulder, roll the fingers toward each other on their knuckles with a double movement, while keeping the fingers in place.

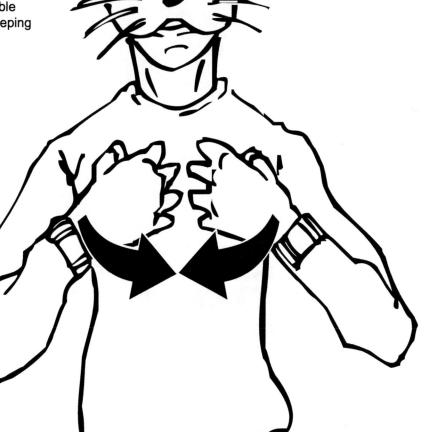

animal – animal

Family, Home, Holidays, & Transportation

87

With the "G" handshape of the dominant hand at the mouth, palm forward, repeatedly open and close the index finger.

[As if displaying a bird's beak]

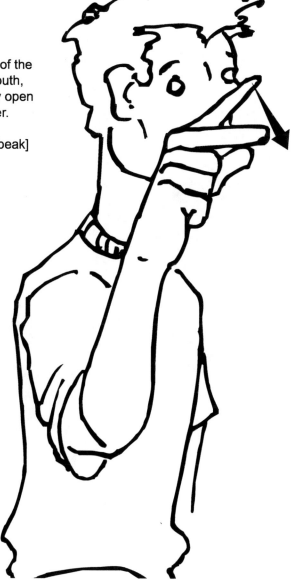

bird - pájaro

Copyright © 2008 Time to Sign, Inc.

88

Family, Home, Holidays, & Transportation

With the "U" handshapes crossed above the wrists, palms facing in and thumbs extended, bend the fingers of both hands forward and back towards the chest with a double movement.

[Indicates the rabbits ears]

bunny, rabbit - conejo

Copyright © 2008 Time to Sign, Inc.

Family, Home, Holidays, & Transportation

The "F" handshapes touch the corners of the upper lips, brushing out and away from the face a couple of times, palms facing each other.

[Indicating a cat's whiskers]

cat – gato

Family, Home, Holidays, & Transportation

Snap the middle finger against the thumb of the dominant hand. Can also add slapping the upper leg.

[As if calling a dog]

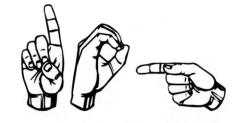

dog – perro

Family, Home, Holidays, & Transportation

While touching the wrist of the dominant open hand, palm facing reference, with the extended reference index finger, swing the dominant hand back and forth with a double movement.

[Like a fish swimming]

fish - pez

Copyright © 2008 Time to Sign, Inc.

Family, Home, Holidays, & Transportation

Begin with the dominant "S" handshape under the chin, knuckles pointing to reference side; flick the index and middle fingers outward with a double movement.

[As if to indicate the filling of air into the frog's throat]

frog – rana

Family, Home, Holidays, & Transportation

With the "H" handshapes beside the temples, palms facing forward, wave the index and middle fingers up and down.

[Indicates a horse's ears]

horse - caballo

Family, Home, Holidays, & Transportation

Flick the extended dominant index finger, palm facing reference, across the tip of the nose with a double movement.

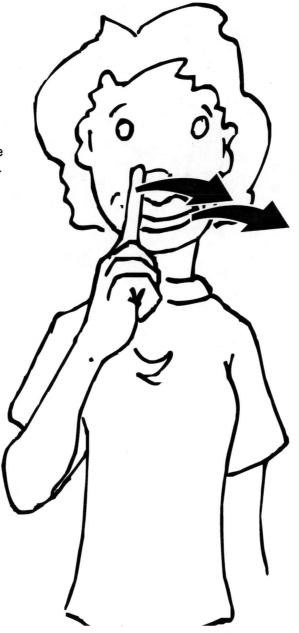

mouse - ratón

Family, Home, Holidays, & Transportation

95

Pull the fingertips of the dominant open hand, palm facing down, and back toward the chest from the fingers to the wrist of the reference open hand, palm facing down, while bending the finger back into the palm.

pets – animales domésticos

Copyright © 2008 Time to Sign, Inc.

Family, Home, Holidays, & Transportation

Hold the bent "V" handshape, palm facing forward, in front of the dominant shoulder, move the hand in a circular motion two times.

snake – serpiente

Copyright © 2008 Time to Sign, Inc.

Family, Home, Holidays, & Transportation

Cup the reference palm over the dominant "A" handshape and wiggle the dominant thumb with a repeated movement.

[As if the turtle's head is coming out of its shell]

turtle – tortuga

Copyright © 2008 Time to Sign, Inc.

Holiday Signs

-

Señales

Feriado

Family, Home, Holidays, & Transportation  99

Bring the dominant open hand, palm facing in, from the chest forward and down, ending with the back of the dominant hand in the upturned palm of the reference open hand. Then with the dominant elbow resting on the back of the reference hand held across the body, palm facing down, bring the extended dominant index finger downward toward the reference elbow in a large arc.

birthday - cumpleaños

Copyright © 2008 Time to Sign, Inc.

Family, Home, Holidays, & Transportation

Begin with the dominant "C" handshape, palm down, over reference arm held across the body, move the dominant hand from the elbow of the reference arm up in an arc.

[Initialized Sign]

Christmas – Navidad

Family, Home, Holidays, & Transportation

101

Begin with both "E" handshapes at the sides of the body, palm facing forward. Move hands in an outward circular motion.

Easter – Pascua

Copyright © 2008 Time to Sign, Inc.

Tap the dominant "5" handshape, palm facing reference side, against the forehead in a double movement. Then with the dominant elbow resting on the back of the reference hand held across the body, palm facing down, bring the extended dominant index-finger downward toward the reference elbow in a large arc.

Father's Day – Día de los Padres

Family, Home, Holidays, & Transportation

Move both curved hands from in front of each eye, palm facing in, and fingers pointing up, around each side of the head, ending with the palms angled forward.

[Also can be done using "H" handshapes]

Halloween - Vispera del Día de todos los Santos

Family, Home, Holidays, & Transportation

Beginning with the little fingers of both "4" handshapes touching in front of the chest, palms facing in and fingers pointing up, move the hands apart in an arc, ending with the hands in front of each shoulder.

Hanukkah - Hanukkah

Family, Home, Holidays, & Transportation

Tap the thumbs of both "5" handshapes near each armpit, palms facing each other and fingers pointing forward, with a double movement.

[Also: vacation]

holiday - día de fiesta

Family, Home, Holidays, & Transportation

Beginning with the wrists of both "I" handshapes crossed in front of the chest, palms facing in, swing the arms apart, ending with the "I" handshapes in front of each shoulder, palms facing forward. Then with the dominant elbow resting on the back of the reference hand held across the body, palm facing down, bring the extended dominant index-finger downward toward the reference elbow in a large arc.

Independence Day - Día de la Independencia

Family, Home, Holidays, & Transportation

Begin with dominant "5" handshape, palm facing forward, then form a "K" handshape with your reference hand, palm facing in, and place the "K" handshape on the heel of the dominant hand.

[You can also Fingerspell: k – w – a – n – z – a – a]

Kwanzaa – Kwanzaa

Family, Home, Holidays, & Transportation

Tap the heel of the dominant "S" handshape, palm facing forward, with a double movement on the back of the reference "S" handshape held in front of the body, palm facing down. Then with the dominant elbow resting on the back of the reference hand held across the body, palm facing down, bring the extended dominant index-finger downward toward the reference elbow in a large arc.

Labor Day – Día del Trabajo

Copyright © 2008 Time to Sign, Inc.

Family, Home, Holidays, & Transportation

Tap the dominant "5" handshape, palm facing reference side, against the chin with a double movement. Then with the dominant elbow resting on the back of the reference hand held across the body, palm facing down, bring the extended dominant index-finger downward toward the reference elbow in a large arc.

Mother's Day – Día de las Madres

Copyright © 2008 Time to Sign, Inc.

Slide the back of the dominant curved handshape, palm facing up, from the fingertips to the heel of the upturned reference open hand. Then beginning with the dominant "S" handshape, palm facing reference side, over the "S" handshape, palm facing right, move the dominant hand forward in a complete circle around the reference hand, ending with the little finger side of the dominant hand on the thumb side of the reference hand.

New Years - Año Nuevo

Family, Home, Holidays, & Transportation

111

Move the dominant "P" handshape in an arc forward across the bent reference hand, palm facing down.

Passover - Festividad de Pésaj

Copyright © 2008 Time to Sign, Inc.

Begin with both "C" handshapes near the sides of the forehead, palms facing forward, move the hands outward to above each shoulder while closing into "S" handshape. Then with the dominant elbow resting on the back of the reference hand held across the body, palm facing down, bring the extended dominant index-finger downward toward the reference elbow in a large arc.

President's Day – el día del Presidente

Family, Home, Holidays, & Transportation  113

Beginning with dominant "S" handshape on top of the reference open palm, move the dominant hand in a curving motion off the reference hand. Then with the dominant "F" handshape on top of the back of the reference hand, move the "F" handshape upward. Then with the dominant elbow resting on the back of the reference hand held across the body, palm facing down, bring the extended dominant index finger downward toward the reference elbow in a large arc.

St. Patrick's Day - Día de San Patricio

Copyright © 2008 Time to Sign, Inc.

Family, Home, Holidays, & Transportation

Touch both hands to the mouth, palms facing in, bring out from the mouth in a double motion.

Thanksgiving - Día de Acción de Gracias

Family, Home, Holidays, & Transportation

115

With both "V" handshapes in front of the body make the shape of a heart starting from the top and working your way to the bottom point. Then with the dominant elbow resting on the back of the reference hand held across the body, palm facing down, bring the extended dominant index finger downward toward the reference elbow in a large arc.

Valentine's Day – Día de San Valentín

Copyright © 2008 Time to Sign, Inc.

Family, Home, Holidays, & Transportation

Transportation Signs

-

Señales De Transportación

Family, Home, Holidays, & Transportation  117

Move the dominant hand with the thumb, index finger, and little finger extended ("I love you" handshape), palm facing down, forward with a short repeated movement in front of the dominant shoulder.

[As if flying an airplane across the sky]

airplane - aeroplano

Copyright © 2008 Time to Sign, Inc.

118

Family, Home, Holidays, & Transportation

Move both "S" handshapes in alternating forward circles, palms facing down, in front of each side of the body.

[As if pedaling a bicycle]

bicycle- bicicleta

Family, Home, Holidays, & Transportation

119

With the little-finger sides of both curved hands together, palms angled slightly apart, move the hands forward in a bouncing double arc in front of the body.

boat - bote

Family, Home, Holidays, & Transportation

Touch the fingertips of the dominant "V" handshape, palm facing reference side, first to the bottom of the wrist and then near the elbow of the reference arm held in front of the chest, palm facing down.

bridge - puente

Family, Home, Holidays, & Transportation

Bring both bent "V" handshapes from in front of each side of the waist, palms facing each other, around to mesh the fingers together in front of the waist.

[As if fastening a seat belt]

buckle - abrochar

Family, Home, Holidays, & Transportation

Beginning with the little-finger side of the dominant "B" handshape touching the index-finger side of the reference "B" handshape, palms facing in opposite directions, move the dominant hand back towards the dominant shoulder.

[Initialized sign]

bus - autobús

Family, Home, Holidays, & Transportation

123

Beginning with both "S" handshapes in front of the chest, palms facing in and the reference hand higher than the dominant hand, move the hands in an up-and-down motion with a repeated alternating movement.

[Mimic driving a car]

[Also: automobile, drive]

car - coche

Copyright © 2008 Time to Sign, Inc.

 **Family, Home, Holidays, & Transportation**

Beginning with both open hands near each shoulder, and fingers angled outward in opposite directions, bend the wrists repeatedly, causing the hands to wave.

[Used to indicate a bird or bug flying]

fly – volar

Copyright © 2008 Time to Sign, Inc.

Family, Home, Holidays, & Transportation

With the extended thumb of the dominant "U" handshape against the dominant side of the forehead, palm facing forward, bend the fingers of the "U" handshape up and down with a double movement. Then with the dominant "V" handshape placed on top of the index-finger side of the reference "B" handshape, palm facing forward, move hand forward.

horseback riding - montar a caballo

Copyright © 2008 Time to Sign, Inc.

126

Family, Home, Holidays, & Transportation

With an alternating movement, move both "A" handshapes forward and back past each other quickly, palms facing each other in front of the body

racing - carreras

Copyright © 2008 Time to Sign, Inc.

Family, Home, Holidays, & Transportation

127

With the fingers of the dominant bent "U" handshape, palm facing down, hooked over the thumb of the reference "C" handshape, palm facing dominant side, move the hands forward in front of the body.

ride - paseo

Start with both "S" handshapes, palms facing each other and slightly down and held in front of either side of the body, move hands in a forward circular motion. Then with the little-finger sides of both curved hands together, palms angled slightly apart, move the hands forward in a bouncing double arc.

rowboat – bote de remos

Family, Home, Holidays, & Transportation

129

Begin with the dominant "B" handshape, palm facing in, against the palm side of the reference "3" handshape, palm facing dominant side, move both hands forward a short distance.

sailboat - bote de vela

Copyright © 2008 Time to Sign, Inc.

Move the dominant "H" handshape from near the dominant shoulder downward towards the reference "H" handshape held in front of the waist until the fingers overlap, both palms facing in.

seatbelt – cinturón

Family, Home, Holidays, & Transportation

131

Begin with the dominant "V" handshape, palm and fingers pointing down, standing on the back of the reference open hand, palm facing down, and move both hands side to side.

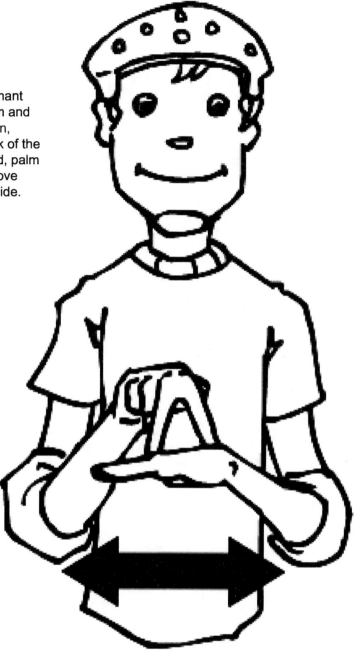

skateboarding - patineta

Copyright © 2008 Time to Sign, Inc.

Family, Home, Holidays, & Transportation

Begin with the back of the dominant bent "V" handshape, palm facing up, across the back of the reference open handshape, palm facing down, push the dominant hand forward.

sledding - trineo

Copyright © 2008 Time to Sign, Inc.

Family, Home, Holidays, & Transportation

Bring the little finger side of the dominant open hand abruptly down on the open reference hand, palm facing up. Then, with both "1" handshapes, palms facing down, draw the outline of a square.

[As if chopping on something]

stop sign - senal de pare

Family, Home, Holidays, & Transportation

Start with both open handshapes, palms facing each other in front of the body. Then move both hands simultaneously forward a short distance.

[shows the outline of a street]

street – calle

**Family, Home, Holidays,
& Transportation**

Bring the little finger side of the dominant open hand abruptly down on the reference palm facing up. Then start with the fingertips of the dominant "8" handshape near the chin, palm facing in, flick the middle finger upward and forward with a double movement each time opening into a "5" handshape.

traffic light – semáforo

Copyright © 2008 Time to Sign, Inc.

136   Family, Home, Holidays, & Transportation

Rub the fingers of the dominant "H" handshape back and forth with a repeated movement on the fingers of the reference "H" handshape held in front of the body, both palms facing down.

train - tren

Copyright © 2008 Time to Sign, Inc.

Family, Home, Holidays, & Transportation

137

Place the little-finger side of the dominant "T" handshape touching the index-finger side of the reference "T" handshape, palms facing opposite directions, move the dominant hand in while moving the reference hand out.

truck - camión

Copyright © 2008 Time to Sign, Inc.

Family, Home, Holidays, & Transportation

Open hands, palms down, are moved in a forward-downward motion alternately

[As if walking with the hands]

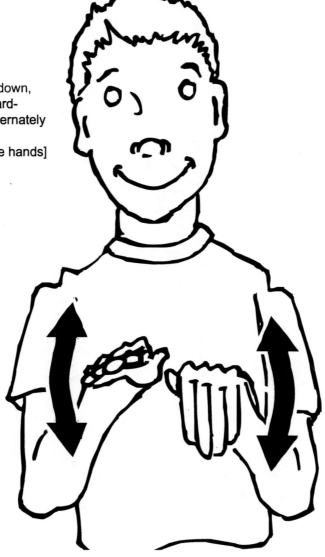

walk - caminar

Family, Home, Holidays, & Transportation

139

Start with the two index-fingers, palms facing in, knuckles facing each other, move the fingers in a rotating circular motion forward.

wheels - ruedas

Copyright © 2008 Time to Sign, Inc.

Start with both index-fingers, fingers pointing up and palms facing each other, move the fingers side to side.

[Represents the movement of windshield wipers]

wipers - limpiabrisas

Family, Home, Holidays, & Transportation

SIGN LANGUAGE HANDOUT PARENTS

What is American Sign Language?

father - padre   mother - madre

- ASL is a language used in the U.S. and Canada that uses no voice. It has its own grammar and language structure (syntax), including: facial grammatical markers, spatial linguistic information, finger spelling, and individual signs.

- ASL is a true and natural language where the sign often mimics the experiences with ideas or objects.

- ASL is NOT derived from any spoken language. It is not based on the English language or any other voiced language.

Incorporate Signing Into Your Child's Daily Routine

- Learn the signs for songs that you sing and sign with your kids.
- Use key signs for story words that you read with your kids.
- Use games to reinforce the learning of signs.
- Use signs for manners whenever appropriate to use manner words.
- Use common signs with school age children, particularly during meal and family times to help them better learn their signs.
- Repetition is key to learning and retention. Sign the key signs each time the words are used.

Copyright © 2008 Time to Sign, Inc.

SIGN LANGUAGE HANDOUT
FAMILY

brother - hermano

family - familia

father - padre

mother - madre

sister - hermana

Family, Home, Holidays, & Transportation

SIGN LANGUAGE HANDOUT
MOTHER'S DAY

happy – feliz   mother - madre   day - día   you - usted

Happy Mother's Day

Happy Mother's Day to you.
Happy Mother's Day to you.
Happy Mother's Day dear Mommy,
Happy Mother's Day to you.

Copyright © 2008 Time to Sign, Inc.

SIGN LANGUAGE HANDOUT
FATHER'S DAY

happy – feliz | father - padre | day - día | you - usted

Happy Father's Day

Happy Father's Day to you.
Happy Father's Day to you.
Happy Father's Day dear Daddy,
Happy Father's Day to you.

Family, Home, Holidays, & Transportation

SIGN LANGUAGE HANDOUT
HOME SIGNS I

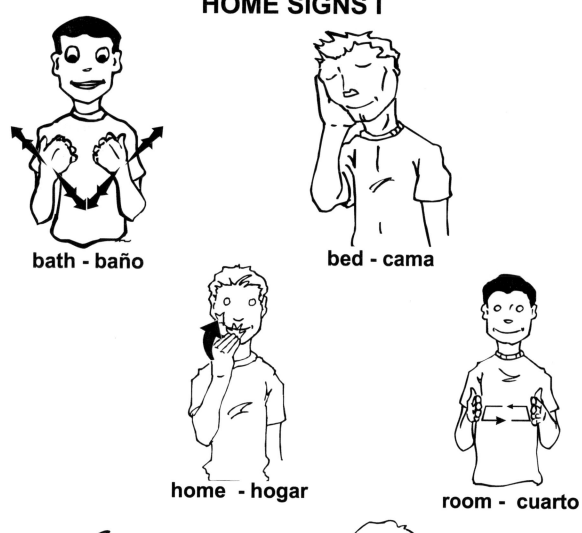

bath - baño

bed - cama

home - hogar

room - cuarto

telephone - telefono

toilet - baño

SIGN LANGUAGE HANDOUT
RELATIVES

aunt - tía

cousin – primo(a)

family - familia

grandfather - abuelo

grandmother - abuela

uncle - tío

Copyright © 2008 Time to Sign, Inc.

SIGN LANGUAGE HANDOUT
PETS I

SIGN LANGUAGE HANDOUT
PETS II

Family, Home, Holidays, & Transportation

149

SIGN LANGUAGE HANDOUT
HOLIDAYS I

**President's Day –
el día del Presidente**

**Valentine's Day -
Día de San Valentín**

**St. Patrick's Day –
Día de San Patricio**

Passover - Festividad de Pésaj

Easter – Pascua

Copyright © 2008 Time to Sign, Inc.

SIGN LANGUAGE HANDOUT
HOLIDAYS II

**Mother's Day –
Día de las Madres**

**Father's Day –
Día de los Padres**

**Independence Day -
Día de la Independencia**

**Labor Day –
día del Trabajo**

birthday - cumpleaños

holiday - día feriado

Copyright © 2008 Time to Sign, Inc.

Family, Home, Holidays, & Transportation

151

SIGN LANGUAGE HANDOUT
HOLIDAYS III

Halloween - Víspera del Día de Todos los Santos

Thanksgiving - Día de Acción de Gracias

Hanukkah - Hanukkah

Christmas - Navidad

Kwanzaa - Kwanzaa

New Years - Nuevo Año

Copyright © 2008 Time to Sign, Inc.

SIGN LANGUAGE HANDOUT
BOATING

boat - bote

bridge - puente

row boat - bote de remos

sail boat - bote de vela

Copyright © 2008 Time to Sign, Inc.

Family, Home, Holidays, & Transportation

SIGN LANGUAGE HANDOUT
TRANSPORTATION I

horseback riding - montar a caballo

racing - carrerra

bicycle - bicicleta

skateboarding - patineta

sled - trineo

walking - cominar

Copyright © 2008 Time to Sign, Inc.

SIGN LANGUAGE HANDOUT
TRANSPORTATION II

Family, Home, Holidays, & Transportation

SIGN LANGUAGE HANDOUT
TRANSPORTATION III

airplane - aeroplano

bus - autobús

fly - volar

train - tren

truck - camión

Copyright © 2008 Time to Sign, Inc.

SIGN LANGUAGE HANDOUT
SAFETY

buckle - abrochar

help - ayuda

safety - seguridad

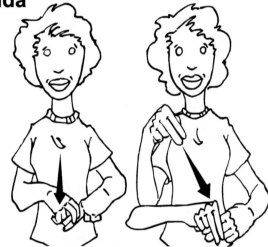
seatbelt - cinturón

stop - parar

traffic light - semáforo

Family, Home, Holidays, & Transportation

INDEX

A

airplane 117, 155
animal 86, 147
aunt 69, 146

B

baby 70
bath 51, 145
bed 52, 145
bicycle 118, 153
bird 87, 147
birthday 99, 150
boat 119, 152
boy 71
bridge 120, 152
brother 72, 142
buckle 121, 156
bunny 147
bunny, rabbit 88
bus 122, 155

C

car 123, 154
cat 89, 147
chair 53
Christmas 100, 151
cousin 73, 146

D

day 143, 144
dog 90, 147
door 54

E

Easter 101, 149

F

family 74, 142, 146
father 75, 141, 142, 144
Father's Day 102, 150
fish 91, 148

fly 124, 155
frog 92, 148

G

girl 76
grandfather 77, 146
grandmother 78, 146

H

Halloween 103, 151
Hanukkah 104, 151
happy 143, 144
help 156
holiday 105, 150
home 55, 145
horse 93, 148
horseback riding 125, 153
house 56
hug 79

I

I love you 80
Independence Day 106, 150

K

kiss 81
Kwanzaa 107, 151

L

Labor Day 108, 150
live 57

M

mother 82, 141, 142, 143
Mother's Day 109, 150
mouse 94, 148

N

New Years 110, 151

Copyright © 2008 Time to Sign, Inc.

INDEX

P

Passover 111, 149
pet 147
pets 95
pillow 58
President's Day 112, 149

R

racing 126, 153
ride 127, 154
room 59, 145
row boat 152
rowboat 128

S

safety 156
sail boat 152
sailboat 129
seatbelt 130, 156
sister 83, 142
skateboarding 131, 153
Skateboarding 131
sled 153
sledding 132
sleepy 61
snake 96
soap 60
stop 156
stop sign 133
St. Patrick's Day 113, 149
street 134, 154

T

table 62
teddy bear 63
telephone 64, 145
Thanksgiving 114, 151
toilet 65, 145
toy 66
traffic light 135, 154, 156
train 136, 155

truck 137, 155
turtle 97, 148

U

uncle 84, 146

V

Valentine's Day 115, 149

W

walk 138
walking 153
wheels 139, 154
window 67
wipers 140, 154

Y

you 143, 144

Alphabet & Numbers Flashcards

These flashcards make learning American Sign Language fun and easy!

Learn the alphabet and numbers signs the fun way!
These fun flashcards are made of sturdy cardstock, and are each 8.5" x 11" for easy viewing. The Animal Alphabet set (26 cards) includes signs for each letter of the alphabet, and also features animals pictures and signs. The Things That Go Numbers set (25 cards) includes signs from 1-20, 100, 1,000, 1 million, as well as dollars and cents, and teaches children modes of transportation signs as well. Both sets feature English, Spanish, and Sign, as well as brightly illustrated pictures and are laminated to 5mil thick to stand up to wear and tear.

Time to Sign inc.™

PO Box 33831
Indialantic, FL 32903
Phone 321.259.0976
www.timetosign.com

Contact us at 321.259.0976 or contact@timetosign.com for more information!